This book is dedicated to Mam,
Nora Gleavey, for all her loving sacrifices

Welcome Home Pat Ruane

by

Mary Gleavey

First Published 1998 by Countyvise, 14 Appin Road, Birkenhead, Wirral, Merseyside L41 9HH, in conjuction with the author Mary Gleavey.
Copyright © 1998 Mary Gleavey.
The right of Mary Gleavey to be identified as the author of this work has been asserted by her in accordance with the Copyright, Designs and Patents Act 1988.
British Library Cataloguing in Publication Data.
A catalogue record for this book is available from the British Library.
ISBN 1 901231 08 9

INTRODUCTION

by

Colin Wilson

I have been so gripped by this moving and fascinating book that I read it from beginning to end in one sitting. It is the life story of Mary Gleavey, an Irish woman whose family came to live on the Mersey, and the core of the book is her 'psychic' experiences, which are told with an honesty and simplicity that is totally convincing.

But what I found so absorbing is not primarily the accounts of paranormal perception, but the warm and oddly engaging personality of the author, as it emerges in the story of her life - anyone who reads a dozen pages will see exactly what I mean.

A few hours before beginning it and old friend who had come to supper commented on a dangerous cliff in Portreath, north Cornwall - where he had just been staying - and remarked that a young soldier had committed suicide from it a few days ago. I said: 'Perhaps he just slipped.' Oh no. He was in debt and was in trouble with the law and his marriage had broken up. . . ' I suddenly felt, with total clarity, that no matter how difficult life becomes, suicide is not the answer. Reading Mary Gleavey' s book underlined that perception. In many ways her life has been hard. After the break-up of her marriage, she had to support herself working at poorly paid - and often part-time jobs. The natural desire for a partner led to a couple of less than satisfactory affairs, in the second of which she ignored the flash of insight that told her that this man should be avoided, and ended by regretting it. As a 'divorcee', her life was of often lonely, and apparently pointless. Yet because of her persistence, courage and resilience, it has all 'come right in the end'. She is the perfect illustration of the thought that drifted through my head as I was listening to the story of the suicide.

I became involved in writing about the 'paranormal' in 1969, when commissioned to write a book about it. My altitude was sceptical almost tongue-in-cheek but as soon as I became absorbed in the subject I became increasingly convinced. Even about life after death - which took me

1

about twenty years to accept I finally came to feel that the balance of scientific evidence is strongly in its favour. But I have always been involved with sceptics - many of them valued friends (for I have never taken intellectual disagreement personally) - who have no doubt that the 'occult' is basically a lot of nonsense and self-deception. As I read, I was aware that they would find half a dozen reasons to explain how Mary Gleavey came to dupe herself into believing that she had had 'psychic' experiences. Yet I would love to present each of them with a copy of this book, and see whether they can honestly believe that she is out to deceive herself or others. To me, every word in it rings true.

Let me mention some of the stories that fascinated me. There is the curious tale of how, when she wanted to accompany a group on holiday to Sweden, she realised that she lacked the money. Then a dream told her the name of as horse that would win the next day. She told her daughter, and they found that the horse was running. It won and at 10 to 1, bringing her the £100 she needed. This is the only time such a thing has happened to her .

I have written elsewhere of three well authenticated cases of precognition involving horse races - I even made a television programme about one of them - and so I have additional reason to believe her story. What does it mean? It's seems to indicate that 'something' (or someone) cared about her enough to give her the money. The alternative explanation is that it was simply a case of 'precognition' - an ability that involved Mary Gleavey alone, and I agree this is an equally valid explanation; but other stories in the book incline me to the first. And if I ask myself why I experience a kind of glow as I read this story, I recognise that it is because it seems to confirm one of my own basic intuitions: that life is not a tale told by an idiot, signifying nothing, but that what we do somehow 'matters' in a larger context.

Another story that moved me has nothing to do with the paranormal. It was simply her recognition, when she went to work in a home for senile patients, that in spite of her own problems, she had every reason to be grateful about her own life that by comparison with these patients, she was immensely fortunate. This touches the most fundamental preoccupation of my own work - the feeling that we always have so many more reasons for being grateful than for being bored and miserable that, logically speaking, boredom and misery should be impossible. A character in

Dostoevsky says that he would rather stand on a narrow ledge forever, in eternal darkness and tempest, than die at once. About to be hanged, the American gangster Charlie Berger looked at the sky and said: 'It is a beautiful world'. If he'd recognised that earlier, he wouldn't have died on the scaffold. Somehow, human beings have got to get up about the 'worms eye view' in which they live most of their lives, and achieve a bird's eye view.

A friend of mine, a brilliant writer and thinker who has never received his due recognition, commented to me the other day that he sometimes feels as if he had won the National Lottery but they were refusing to give him the money. I sympathise, yet feel he is still leaving something out of account. In my own case 'fame' came at 24 with my first book The Outsider yet, I found that becoming a "celebrity" and a bestseller a far from agreeable experience. It was like being bathed in a spotlight and watched by a huge audience, and as I wrote my next book, it felt as awkward and uncomfortable as having a television crew filming you on a visit to the lavatory. Eighteen months later, my second book, Religion and the Rebel, was 'torn to pieces' yet oddly enough, I felt relieved. They had turned off the spotlight. The other day I re-read much of Religion and the Rebel, and realised that it is an unsatisfactory book because I was writing it in a state of uncomfortable self-awareness, which vanished as soon as the book was hammered into the ground by the critics. Writers like Dickens, Shaw and Wells never escaped the spotlight, and therefore 'jammed' at a certain level of self-development. Mary Gleavey's book confirms my own feeling that our estimation of what, is good and bad for us is comically unreliable.

Mary has no doubt what ever about life after death - she has had far too many experiences that confirm it. In a sense, this seems to me unimportant. I was not particularly convinced by the evidence for life after death in 1970, when I wrote The Occult, and I gradually became convinced over the years as I studied the evidence. But it has made no practical difference to my life; there is a sense in which I don't give a damn. And I feel that, on the whole, it should make no practical difference to most people whether there is life after death. Our problem is to make sense of this life, and to live as purposefully and creatively as we can. Pleasant experiences - like Mary Gleavey's visit to her brother in Australia - make it easier to live with optimism and purpose but our task is to do it anyway. I found extremely significant her story of getting a job as a caretaker in an idyllic place with a castle, where she lived the kind of life that, young poet's dream about. Yet reading a biography of Aneurin Bevan was enough to make her suddenly realise that lotus eating in these pleasant surroundings was not what life was all about, and that she had to get; back in touch with the real world - like the Shaw character who says: 'I don't want to be happy, I want to be alive and active.' It is this kind of insight that, for me, makes the book so rewarding.

I have not even touched on what Mary Gleavey probably feels the most important part of this book - her longstanding misery about the violence in Northern Ireland, her odd premonitions about going there, and her insight that a tragedy involving children - and the intervention of the United States - would be instrumental in starting the peace process. And although I can see that my sceptical friends would shake their heads about her conviction that some psychically-directed power of love can aid the peace process, I again experience a curious lift of the heart at the implication that we human beings can do something purposeful, even about the most terrible situations. It is this feeling, which I experienced constantly as I read, that made this book such a delight to read.

Immediately after finishing it, I decided to write this introduction - although she has certainly not even suggested it - in the hope that it might persuade some publisher that Mary Gleavey deserves to reach a far wider audience.

WELCOME HOME PAT RUANE

I write this story for my grandchildren, who have at this time of writing just spent a heartwarming holiday with me at my present home in Germany.

It is, by way of an explanation for why I have spent a lot of time away from them for some years now.

In truth my thoughts were never far away from them and my two daughters, mother, sisters and brothers. I have driven thousands of miles to see them regularly but missed them always. In my fifties now and far from my roots I seem to have been relieved of a self-imposed burden that I have carried for years, almost to the point of obsession.

The house feels empty now that they have gone home to England. I rattle around alone in the large rooms still full of the memories of their chatter and laughter.

From my kitchen window I can see the snowman that they built in the large garden just made for children to play and romp in.

The snowman's hair was made of green fronds of fern, splashed brightly against the pure, stark whiteness of the freshly fallen snow. The eyes were two bright blue plastic balls placed neatly in its head.

I watched as a young German couple stopped to look, smiling at the splendid, comic figure.

Wistfully, I wished that they were still here as I remembered their excitement as the huge flakes of snow fell and they had played outside until the night was dark and crisp cold and the sky was lit with silvery stars.

Throughout the holiday we had shared much laughter on their first trip abroad. It had all gone too quickly, alas.

I smiled to myself as I remembered how the seven year old had been teased by the twelve and fifteen year old. He tried to tell them a joke and they refused to co-operate with him.

"Knock, knock!" he said.

"Come in!" they kept chanting.

"No", he said frustratedly. "You don't say that!"

Deliberately the two eldest kept winding him up until he was in tears and he came running to his mother and myself.

"They won't listen to my joke" he wailed.

"Never mind we'll listen" I said to mollify him.

"Knock, knock!" he said again.

"Who's there? we called loudly.

"Bear", he replied.

"Bear who?" we said dutifully.

"Bear bum!" he shouted gleefully.

His mother and I roared with laughter.

"See!" he said running back to the others. "They laughed at my joke"

Moments like this were pure gold in family life and now that I was alone again I wondered why on earth my time was being spent in Germany when my heart and mind was in Merseyside with my mother and sisters and brother, not far from North Wales, where five of my grandchildren lived with one of my daughters.

Germany with its pristine, orderly cleanliness seemed vaguely sterile in contrast to Widnes with its belching smoke. An industrial huddle on the banks of the River Mersey. A town of noxious vapours from the sprawling chemical industries that turned the town from a rural hamlet into a fume ridden environment for the human inhabitants, many of them Irish who had fled from the potato famine to work in this particular part of Lancashire.

In spite of all that I have seen over my travels of latter years, my heart is there with my own people. Their endurance and ability to laugh is unique. A sharp contrast to unsmiling German faces who do not respond to the smiles of strangers. Sit next to someone on a bus in Widnes and you know their life story before they get off. They are so open and friendly, so warm in comparison to the stiff, unyielding Germans. I yearned to go HOME again now. To be in the bosom of my family. But first for my grandchildren I tell them my story.

Life at No 7 Caroline Street was a particularly crowded, hotch potch affair.

Home was in a row of terraced streets, slap bang in front of the Gas Yard and numerous divisions of the chemical industries that adjoined the banks of the River Mersey in Widnes, Lancashire.

A 'two and a bit' up and a 'two and a bit' down. Two main bedrooms and a tiny box room upstairs and a parlour, kitchen and small scullery downstairs. 'Parlour' was a grand name for an icy cold room with rotting floor boards. Every time you tried to put a shilling in the gas or electric meter you put your life in your hands.

At the end of the cobbled yard at the back of the house was a flush toilet (sometimes it flushed). I suspect it was newspaper that blocked all these toilets, as at that time soft toilet paper was an unheard of luxury. Probably the 'Widnes Weekly News' was responsible for more blocked drains than readers. It certainly served as a table cloth in many homes.

Also in the back yard was a concrete Air Raid Shelter that an enterprising uncle had made during the war years.

For Patrick Gleavey and Nora (nee McCarthy) and their seven children it was a bit squashed to say the least.

Caroline Street was one of many terraced housed streets built for the mainly Irish and Irish descent workers who worked in the chemical industry. It was as near to Ireland as one could get. Families with names like Muldoon, Riley, O'Shea, Flanagan, Murphy and Cassidy and many more. It was a little bit of Ireland with an Irish culture and strong Roman Catholic foundations in every flagstone and kerb of the narrow, bustling streets.

St Maries Church and the clergy took care of the parishioners' souls and hearts. The Imperial Chemical Industry provided the money to feed the bellies and wet the throats of the hard working chemical labourers and their large families.

They were hard drinkers these men, whose clogs would clatter down their respective back yards in the early morning and in the evening would clatter back coated in white dust. The back entry in the middle of the back to back houses, full of cloth capped men with 'mutton cloth' scarves wound around their necks. These same entries were used for the betting transactions on horse racing with illegal 'bookies'. A mad scuffle, with men running and disappearing into back gates, when a 'look out' sighted the Police, was common place. It even added an excitement to the harsh, unlovely conditions without even a blade of grass in the whole area.

One had to go to the marsh area beside the Mersey and adjoining 'The Cut', a canal linking Widnes to Warrington to find any grass. Even a few cows grazed there although I suspect the quality of the grazing was suspect too.

The men played 'Pitch and Toss' there, a game involving the throwing of coins. Many a pinafored woman with folded arms stood sentry there on pay day to protect her husband's wages.

I have a memory of dark haired, handsome Irish looking young men, vibrant with life and flashing smiles, scattering and vanishing from these ventures whenever their 'game' was threatened. It was a respite from the harshness of their working lives.

There was little or no protective clothing worn in those days although they worked amongst dangerous chemicals. Many men, like my father, had hacking coughs, as did quite a lot of the children living in the noxious fumes. He was really a bit of an invalid with a heart weakness and stomach ulcers, although in his younger days he loved playing Rugby League. Widnes was famous for its Rugby League players - they were all local boys. It was inbred in the boys as were politics in all of us. It was a strong Labour movement town. I can remember waiting in the Town Hall Square with my parents and brothers and sisters. The children would be on the men's shoulders, for the results of a General Election and the whole town would be crammed into the Square alongside the Co op singing "Vote, vote, vote for Mr Shawcross. He's as steady as a rock" It was infectious and fervent, not half-hearted like it is today.

My father was a strict disciplinarian and staunchly Roman Catholic, with no tolerance at all for any other religion or creed. I think even in those early years for me that this 'felt wrong'. It bothered me. The bigotry of the area, with the priests worse than anyone else.

9

The priests and nuns patrolled the streets collecting coppers for the Church. They tried to rule their flock with a rod of iron. In our house the 'Catholic Times' was on the sideboard and the 'News of the World' was under the settee. Converts from the Protestant faith were just tolerated. My grandmother, Mam's mother was one but I heard my father mutter about the 'Orange Woman' more than once. It was in a very definite atmosphere of religious intolerance in which we Gleavey's grew up.

The sermons from the pulpit were Fire and Brimstone and one incident that stuck in my mind was when a young girl married a Protestant boyfriend in a Registry Office. The Priest thundered and raged from the pulpit that this girl was 'No more married than a dog in the street'. Incidents like this always made me sad because I knew that this was wrong.

The best thing that I can say about it really is that there was in all the neighbourhood a very strong family feeling with lots of aunts and uncles with much warmth and love for one another. Nothing was secret. Most of our lives were lived out on the streets. Women would sit out on chairs on the doorstep. Children played endless street games. There were feuds and drunken brawls. Even an element of madness when a poor old man danced naked in the street amongst all the children with a heavy wooden clock in his hands.

Women gossiped and their front doors were always open. They knew everything about one another. Doors were never locked even at night. No-one had anything worth stealing to be honest. There were whispered remarks about 'such-a-body' who 'should have a red light over the door' that I didn't understand until years later. When a woman was in labour with a new offspring, someone would go into the home with plates of food. If there was a death someone in the neighbourhood would 'lay them out' in their parlour. Everyone including children would traipse through to view the body. It was quite common for a child to look curiously at some poor soul with cotton wool stuffed up into their nostrils and with a saucer of salt placed on their chest. A group of people would stay up with the deceased all night. They called it a 'wake'.

By far the most overworked woman in the district was Nurse Smith, the midwife. She brought most of the children into the world as she pedalled up and down on her 'sit up and beg' bicycle with the black box on the back. I always thought that she brought the baby in that box. The birth rate was high and so was poverty.

My dad's suit was one of many items that were in and out of the Pawnshop like a yoyo but there was one pub, even two on some street corners. In retrospect, for the men, an hour in the pub would have been a welcome relief from the toil of work and the abundance of children.

I think that the women understood this. There is many a time I remember my mother scraping a few coppers together for my dad to 'have a pint'. It was the men's club where they talked about politics and rugby league and relaxed after the day's work. Now I can see that.

Pubs and chipshops were plentiful. In my latter years I have eaten at some sumptuous tables but there is nothing that sticks in my mind more than sitting on the doorstep as a child with 'a mixture in a basin, liberally covered in salt and vinegar. A 'mixture' was chips and sloppy peas. If you took a basin and got the chips in the bottom with the peas on the top it was Heaven! I can remember it now. Food of the Gods! That and Savoury Ducks swimming in gravy. My mother would take a basin to Charlie Bills, the butcher, and bring them back and make her own chips with them. Nancy Cassidy had the Chip Shop. Potatoes certainly were our staple diet. I can imagine the hardship and anguish caused to our ancestors in Ireland during the Potato Famine. It was no wonder that so many people had fled. Most people in 'Newtown', the area in which I lived, came from this stock and the Irish ways were still prevalent.

My grandmother, Mary Jane McCarthy had 'second sight' and she used to read the tea leaves. She would never read them for her family but she was very popular with neighbours because of this ability.

I seem to have picked this up from her and often received flashes of clairvoyance. The very first flash I remember vividly. I was playing Hopscotch in the street in the middle of the road which had very little traffic in those days, just the Co-op Milk horse and cart or Spud Murphy's vegetable lorry delivering to Molly Donegan's cat-smelling fruitshop. Molly had a permanent crust of snuff around her nostrils as did Patsy her long-suffering husband. Molly was a very strong minded woman.

I was playing with the chalk in my hand when I had a very vivid impression of Pat Ruane. He was Mrs Ruane's eldest son. He was a sailor and he had been away from home for a long time. For some inexplicable reason I wrote in huge letters on her doorstep "WELCOME HOME PAT RUANE". Pat Ruane arrived home unexpectedly on that doorstep in the early hours of the next morning. The first thing that he saw when he arrived was my greeting.Our household was woken up very early by one of the Ruane children who had brought a big bag of sweets for me. "Thank God it hadn't rained" I thought as I munched on the sweets.

When I was still quite young I had a vivid experience that with the knowledge that I have now, I think was an 'Out of the Body' experience. I can remember clearly standing at the bedroom window on a nice summer evening, totally wide awake and nowhere near sleep. I watched other children playing outside and was peeved because I had been sent to bed. One moment I was watching the children playing and although I swear that I never left that window, inexplicably the next moment I awoke with a start as I heard my Mother shouting us the next morning to get up for school. I swear that I never left that window. Somehow I 'knew' that I had been somewhere else but I had no memory of it and just felt confused and shaken.

My eldest daughter, Lesley, said that she regularly had these experiences as a child but when I tried to tell my family they seemed to think that I was queer. Our Nora, my sister, always thought that I was queer. She still does as a matter of fact!

Mostly in those days I suppose my abilities of second sight were confined to a strange sort of 'inner knowledge'.

I knew when things were going to happen to me, like when I sat for a scholarship to a commercial college. I 'knew' even before I looked at the exam papers that I would win a place. On its own that didn't mean much and lots of the incidents were trivial and concerned mostly myself.

One event however was not so. I was having a conversation with someone who asked me "What would your Dad say if you wanted to marry a Protestant?" I said calmly "He won't be here". I knew that my father would not live to see me married.

Like all teenagers, there was conflict between us. He held such rigid views at that time. I often think that if he had lived longer that he would have mellowed. He died in his fifties. He was older than my mother and never even knew one of his grandchildren. His health and the harsh working conditions robbed him of this. I feel sad that maybe we couldn't have become better friends whilst he was alive. Over the years conditions changed in Widnes. The slums were pulled down, the people rehoused in better homes and the bigotry of the Irish ghetto faded. How he would have enjoyed his grandchildren of which he would now have many.

The person to whom I said "He won't be here" was horrified. "That's an awful thing to say", but I knew, I really did know that my father would not live to see us all grown. I was between seventeen and eighteen when it did happen. The youngest child of us seven was still a baby. I was the eldest. It became a harsh reality, especially for my Mam.

It was quite a revelation to me when at thirteen years of age I did win the scholarship to be trained in commercial and office skills for two years. A uniform was necessary of which I was very proud but it must have taken a lot of ingenuity and struggle for Mam and Dad to provide it.

There were only four Catholics in our class of thirty. The rest of the girls were from better areas of the town. It was a shock to me to realise that these girls had been living in a totally different environment from me. They were more polished, confident and as I made friends and visited their homes I saw that their families were smaller. They lived in more

None of the teaching staff were Catholic either, well, maybe one was. So of course I found out for myself that Protestants were very nice, tolerant people with no fiery religious views and no fear of God whatsoever, for even the slightest misdemeanour.

The Catholic Church thrived on fear. I can remember our Ann as a very young child getting into a lot of trouble because once in Confession, struggling to think of a sin that she had committed said "Forgive me Father for I have committed adultery". There was hell to pay. Instead of smiling and being amused at an obvious child's error she was mortified with shame and still didn't know what she had said. We laugh about it now, of course.

Anyway, amongst these surroundings a whole new world opened up for me away from the insular religious atmosphere of the Parish of St Maries and the rows of back to back houses.

After the two year course I started work as a clerk-typist in a Glass Bottle company in St Helens. St Helens was some miles away and it meant an early morning start as I travelled in daily by bus and after nearly two years of this I heard of a vacancy in the local newspaper office "The Widnes Weekly News". It was poorly paid but I loved it. Printing fascinated me. All the various departments from Compositor's to Machine Room, Bindery and Stereotype department. I was even, a few times, allowed to work on a Linotype Machine. I really loved working there. I would have liked to have become an Ace Reporter but my training was for office work in the General Office. I didn't have the right qualifications to work as a Reporter.

It was at seventeen years of age that my Father died. To this day I will never forget my mother's shocked, stunned face at the graveside. I don't think that it was until that exact moment that she realised that she had been left on her own to bring up seven children. There was me, Mary, Nora, Ann, Patrick, Edward, Christine and Marie Julie, still a baby, who had been named after an aunt who was a nun.

I remember her face turned white and she seemed to crumple. She all but fell on the coffin as it was being lowered into the ground. "My God" she cried "What will I do?"

What a tremendous task she had in front of her to be a mother, father and breadwinner to seven children. How hard it must have been for her. She found work. She had to work. Life must have been an endless treadmill of work for her in those days. She took in washing, she cleaned and worked in factory canteens and until she was sixty years of age she did shift work in a potato crisp factory. Her fingers are permanently closed now. Her tendons, worn out, doctors say, with hard work. She never married again. Who would take on such a large family?

I can never repay her for the way that she toiled for us all and to this day if she has a few bob in her pocket she can't wait to give it away to us, her family. MAM! In those days a Mam had to be a very strong woman. I can never think of her without a rush of love and gratitude.

Soon after I was married to my long term boyfriend, who was a Protestant, I left my job with the newspaper. Dad was not there now to protest about his religion, although the clergy did. To no avail. I would not be browbeaten and I had learned a thing or two by that time. We had both saved our money and had put a deposit on a small semi-detached house in a better part of town.

Within two and a half years we had two beautiful daughters. I can remember their childhood as being the happiest time of my life for me.

At this time of writing they have their own partners and are leading their own lives but every day I miss them and try to see them as often as I can.

We both worked hard, my husband and myself, to build a better lifestyle for them and I fitted in with the children's welfare a variety of jobs. I tackled anything that I could find.

I worked in a chemist's shop. I was a dinner lady, a temporary office cleaner in the Social Security Office. I remember thinking how odd it was that the chairs in the interview rooms were bolted to the floor, until I found out that it was quite common for chairs to be thrown at the clerks by disgruntled claimants. I know how these people must have felt, after sitting on one of those chairs during hard times but in those days work was plentiful and I did not mind what I did as long as it fitted in with my children's school hours.

15

Ann and Julie

Christine and Julie

Myself aged 18 years.

Brother-in-Law Tommy Lowe

Ann, Aunt Molly and Eileen King

17

It became a family joke that 'Mary' had worked in more back yards than a bin man and I suppose that I did.

By far the worst job that I ever did. It was physically hard and unpleasant, was as a lathe operator in an asbestos factory. The pay was good and married women were allowed time off during school holidays and if a child was ill there was no fuss over lost time.

No wonder! It was a terrible job! Around fifty people worked in a long shed-like building without windows, only occasional panels of glass, set into the slanting roof. Considering all the fuss now about safety precautions and health hazards with asbestos, all that I can say is, at the time, there was no concern for health or safety. Asbestos dirt was in the eyes, the ears, the nose and throat and consequently the lungs of people who worked there.

On the section that I worked, asbestos pipes had to be lifted on to a lathe and the conduit section, attached to the end of the pipe had to be filed smoothly by a heavy metal, hand held file, as the lathe swiftly rotated the drainpipe. The pipe had then to be rubbed with emery paper to smooth and clean it. The only protection given, for the hands only, was rubber gloves which were torn to shreds within seconds.

The pipes were of varying sizes. From domestic drainpipes to huge, heavy, underground gas pipes. They were kept in large stock piles and we had to load these pipes onto large 'bogeys' and and then push them to the lathe to clean them.

Some of the women were quick and crafty and managed to get the small pipes first. I always seemed to end up with the heavy gas pipes. It was back breaking, heavy manual work and I hated it in that hot shed with no sunlight. Just noise and dust and hard labour. I remember thinking that 'HELL' must have been very similar.

Doggedly I stuck to it for the money but for a 'softie' used to office work it was very hard for me. My smart office clothes had been exchanged for a filthy apron, rubber gloves, torn to shreds and tatters and a sweaty overall. I prayed that no-one would see me that knew me well.

One thing that really riled me, I can remember, is that when we went to the factory canteen to order a meal, we were refused cutlery with which to eat it. Cutlery was only given to office staff. If we wanted cutlery, we had to bring our own from home. We were not entitled to such luxuries. God! I was livid! I was amazed that after working so hard in such dreadful conditions that we could be treated in such a manner.

My name could have been Mary Scargill because I let it be known just what I thought about it. I learned to stick up for myself alright.

The material quality of our lives prospered and the children never really lacked for anything. We moved to a larger semi in a quieter road where the children played in safety and made friends.

My job in the asbestos factory came to an abrupt end one day when one of the heavy gas pipes crushed one of my hands in a painful accident. There were no bones broken but my hand was very swollen and bruised.

Hilary & Lesley on holiday in Scotland

I admitted defeat and gave up the job that was far too heavy for a woman anyway.

So, what next! Yes, then I started to work for a catering firm as a silver service waitress.

That crude comment "If you stick a brush up my arse I'll sweep the floor as well!" was very apt. A band of women worked for the company who catered for Masonic and Rotary Club functions etc, as well as for weddings and other celebrations.

The waitresses had to do everything. Lay the tables, silver serve the meal, clear away, wash up, serve drinks at the bar, wash glasses and finally clean the kitchens and mop the floors until exhausted we were driven home in the firm's van after, often, a fifteen hour shift with very little rest breaks and very poor wages.

The very first time that I did a Saturday, running from wedding to wedding, I felt that I had been run over by a bus!

Most of the banqueting halls were in the Liverpool area. So different from Widnes, which was more a Lancashire town. The humour of the Liverpool women however was so funny. Their richness of wit and raucous warm hearts alleviated much of the toil. Slavery wasn't dead, even thirty years ago!

When I think of all the jobs that I had then, It is hard to think that there is so much unemployment now. Work was plentiful in those days, if you didn't mind what you did. Exploitation was rife though too!

A brief spell back at my old job in the newspaper office was followed by a move about fifty miles away into North Wales. We moved into a seventeenth century cottage. The cottage was beautiful although my two daughters had mixed feelings. There were however marriage problems. It is not my intention to hurt anyone in these pages so there is much I would like to keep private and my own restlessness I am sure was a lot to blame.

The marriage ended in that cottage, where one night I awoke and saw a young child, a little girl standing by the side of my bed. She was

Lilac Cottage, N. Wales

smaller than my own children and seemed to be searching for something, possibly a non-existent drawer. She was there only briefly. I did not mention this at all. I thought maybe that it was just my imagination. My eldest daughter however saw the same child a few weeks later. We both saw her just the once and never again but it was an interesting rather than a frightening experience.

We parted and my eldest daughter married very young. My younger daughter circulated between us both.

I left the home and so started on numerous temporary homes trying to 'go it alone'. It wasn't easy. I still worked doing whatever I could.

There then began a strange period in my life which started off when I went with two colleagues to a Spiritualist Church. I forget now who actually suggested it. We just thought that it would be a 'lark'.

It was a strange sort of set up. A tatty back room really. Not very big, with a table cum altar with flowers in vases, a hymn book and rows of plain wooden chairs. It smelt a bit musty and the whole effect was shabby.

21

We avoided looking at each other in case we giggled. I was just curious but faintly repelled by the whole scene. The congregation consisted of middle aged and elderly women with just a few men.

I didn't know what to expect from the elderly man who was running the show that night. He was introduced to us by a lady as 'The Medium'. I was flabbergasted when he addressed himself to me. He said that he had my father with him. I rather doubted that my father, a staunch Roman Catholic, would turn up in a back room in North Wales.

Had I recently changed my hairstyle? He said my father liked it. I nodded and said "Yes" still being unimpressed. Then to my complete astonishment he said that he had Mary Jane with him. Mary Jane was my clairvoyant grandmother. He then relayed a verbal bandinage between them that was so typical of them in their lifetime. They were still sniping at each other. It was amazing. From what he said I was convinced that somehow the Medium had communicated to me a conversation from my father and grandmother. I was amazed but still puzzled as to how something so wonderful could be happening in such a shabby place.

Excitedly I read everything that I could find on Psychic Research which usually included Spiritualism. I made an absolute pest of myself by insisting that everyone that I knew shared in my new found knowledge.

I went to other churches and was given a favourite Aunt of mine named Molly and very often there was more from my father and grandmother. Even my paternal grandmother whom I had never known was mentioned. It was told to me that when she was alive she had one leg shorter than the other. When I checked with family, this had been true.

I have to admit that the evidence was not always good. Some mediums I am sure deluded themselves that they were mediums. Nevertheless the times when the evidence was good was fairly frequent and I was convinced that there was something in it. For a while it was like a drug to me, this knowledge that people could communicate after death and I became absorbed by it.

Someone suggested that I talk to a lady, a chiropodist, a lovely natured woman who was reputed to be a Healer.

To be frank, when I went to see her and she sat me in her chiropodist chair and held my feet whilst she said that she saw this and heard that, I thought she was a bit barmy. Her eyes were closed all the time and I couldn't hear anything.

I couldn't get out of the chair and that surgery quickly enough. I ran from the room like a bat out of hell and told myself that I would not involve myself in such queer 'goings on'. It was a strange and odd experience. Little did I know that it was to be the first of many strange experiences.

Next morning as I lay in bed on the verge of waking fully I had my very first vivid Psychic Vision. I saw a brightly coloured scenario in a symbolic form and I heard a voice, male, very cultured and gentle saying to me "There you are now, get better".

I wasn't aware of it at the time but 'He' was showing me the future played out in a symbolic form. Later when these events happened I realised what I had been shown. My interest therefore did continue as I realised that something very unusual was happening to me.

I didn't think of it as a religious experience. I have never and still do not go overboard on organised religion but as I lived alone then for most of the time and found the loneliness crippling after coming from a large family with little privacy, I became committed to an investigation into Psychic Research.

The chiropodist, who became a friend, suggested that as I was a little Psychic myself that I should join a Developing Circle with about half a dozen psychic people who were known to her.

So began a fascinating period in my life.

The leader of the group, we were all female, would 'open up' with a short prayer. Just something simple. Not too heavy or anything. Then she would invite unseen sources to communicate with us. We would then sit in complete silence for half an hour with our eyes closed. The leader would then invite each member to say what they had seen and heard during the silence.

Well, what the others had seen and heard was nobody's business as they related this, that and the other. Some of them apparently had seen wonderful things. I saw nothing and continued to see nothing for a long time.

Frankly, I was peeved and thought that they were all making it up and wondered if they weren't all more than a bit 'cracked'. Eventually however I did begin to experience clairvoyant episodes and gave the others clairvoyant messages. My communications were straight out with no messing. No fancy, airy fairy frills generally future events for the people with me in the room. So my sorely tried patience paid off. I attended these sessions every week and enjoyed them.

My dreaming became very lucid and I began to dream the week's events in one dream. The whole week's experiences would be played in one continuous film as if only one event. So in that way it was a little scrambled. The only thing was, that if anything bad happened, or if I had a big disappointment, I had to experience it twice, once, in a dream and then once when it really happened. My senses were definitely heightened.

One night, however, the dream was exceptionally clear. I was due to go on a four day trip to Sweden with some friends and as the day grew nearer, I realised that I would not be able to go. I was finding it hard to manage financially. There seemed to be no way that I could find the money to go. Very down, one night as I went to bed I fell asleep knowing that my trip could not be done. As I slept I dreamt of a Horse Race. I was shown a horse, was told its name and was urged to place a bet on it as it would win. It was so real!

My youngest daughter was with me that night and next morning I told her of my dream. We bought a newspaper to see if a horse of that name was running. It was!

Anxiously I put my last £10 on it and won £100. Just about the price of the trip. This caused quite a stir amongst my colleagues at work. They waited eagerly for me every morning to see if I had dreamed about any more winners. They analysed my dreams with very obscure interpretations relating to the runners at Chepstow etc but it never happened again. I was never meant, obviously, to win again.

On the trip to Sweden with friends.

The trip was magical. I had only been abroad once before to Majorca with my ex-husband. Sweden was beautiful. I stood watching the wake behind the ship as we sailed marvelling at the vastness of the sea and sky and silently thanked my unseen benefactor who had made the trip possible.

After spending the first twenty years of my life in a 'back to back' terraced street travel excited me tremendously.

It was a fun trip with lots of laughter. Sweden was a picture of majestic loveliness with soft Autumn colours and a pristine cleanliness. It was magic and I was so grateful for the opportunity that had been given to me in such a strange way.

God Bless Saddle Tramp!

and all who win on her!

After my trip to Sweden my sense of inner loneliness increased. Many hours were spent in solitary isolation, apart from regular contact with my daughters.

25

I was doing clerical work for the Health Authority and I remember the very first day that I had started this job. I was introduced to a man who had himself started to work there on the same day. As I shook hands with him a voice in my head said quite clearly "This will be the next man in your life!" I was startled. I was still married at the time and he was older than I was and on first impressions of him I privately thought that it was very unlikely, so I had forgotten about it.

He was an ebullient man who enjoyed life to the full and in my heart although I knew that it was very unwise, like a moth that is drawn towards a flame, knowing full well that it will bring destruction, I was drawn to him. During those years I really did crave affection.

This man was a warm and loving man. He spread his warmth far and wide however and that brought a lot of heartache and unhappiness. I suppose that he was a typical opportunist who loved women and cheated and lied to them all.

One wonders just how much fate does play a part in these things. I certainly felt that I could not avoid this friendship. I was drawn into it like a whirlpool.

With hindsight now I can look back and think positively about what I gained from the experience and I know that he gave me affection, gentleness and a kindness that I had never known in my life. He was a kindly man and I needed his softness and apparent enjoyment of female company. He was not capable of making a commitment to anyone but I realise now how lonely women must have loved him. He gave them tenderness even if just for a few moments.

He became very ill with cancer and suffered a long and lingering death. It was heartbreaking to see this man who loved life so much become painfully thin and wracked with pain. Many people, male and female, were fond of him. He lit up a room when he came into it with his humour, his energy. He was a very vibrant person and we were all sad to witness his demise.

I still regularly went back to Widnes to visit my mother and it was in her living room as I sat reading a book that I saw him illuminated in the doorway. It was rather like a hologram, not a full flesh and blood figure.

He was illuminated as if on a different frequency with an aura around him of pale colours. He looked, not as I had last seen him, gaunt and wasted. He looked beautiful, more like his old self. It didn't last long, maybe thirty seconds and then it faded.

I noted the time on the clock. Later that night I had a telephone call to say that he had died at that same time. In spite of all the heartache it was a privilege to have witnessed such a beautiful goodbye.

My husband at about this time had sold our previous home and being a fair man he gave me some of the accumulated equity. It wasn't a lot but I had given up my clerical job and was just drifting and restless.

I had heard of a Psychic College in Stansted in Essex and decided to go on a course there. During the day I attended lectures, demonstrations and workshops and my interest deepened in the whole area of metaphysics and mysticism and I had some very good sittings there from various Mediums. Their knowledge of my life and events could not have been dismissed as guesswork by any means.

It was in the beautiful library there during a Meditation Session that I saw with startling clarity my father, Patrick Gleavey, walking towards me. I must have gasped aloud because I remember the Medium murmuring softly to me. He was not alone. I assume that it must have been a 'Guide' with him - he was a young, attractive man in Arab dress. I can still remember clearly the rope around his waist. It was brown silk. There was such a feeling of love from my father. It made me feel so peaceful and serene. No words were spoken.

Why my father had this Arab with him I don't know. I was not and never have been one of these Psychics who have 'Sitting Bull' etc accompanying them on their every move. I always tried to be scrupulously honest and avoided exaggeration.

The love and affection came to me in waves from my father. The colours were vivid. In life at times my father had seemed such a stern and unapproachable man; he had been a 'tartar' at times and if I am to be completely honest, if I had wanted to bring someone to communicate with me, it would not have been him. My surprise therefore was great and the love he sent indisputable. It was very moving for me.

My return to Wales was filled again with seasonal work and depressing accommodation but I met regularly with psychic friends. Permanent work now was getting hard to find and again I did everything that I could find. I wore a red blazer as a Club Receptionist in a Holiday Camp, worked in snack bars, swimming pools, all during the summer months.

One winter with a permanently heavy heart and struggling with black depression I decided to take a little of my money and take a trip to Australia to see my brother, Patrick, who had been over there for years.

The whole experience was fantastic. It had been about fifteen years since any of us had seen my brother, Patrick, who had gone to Australia to build a better life. I knew that my mother fretted for him so I asked her to come along. She was very frightened of such a long journey, and would not go. So feeling very extravagant in the circumstances I went alone.

I could not really believe that I, Mary Gleavey, was really standing in Bombay and Kuala Lumpa when the plane stopped to refuel. Even though I was enjoying these exotic sights alone, it was still adventurous and exciting.

At Perth Airport I panicked when I saw the sea of faces waiting in Arrivals as I pushed my trolley through the lounge. What if I didn't recognise him after all this time? I needn't have worried. A big bear of a man ran forward and picked me up bodily, tears running down his face. It was a beautiful moment. Our Pat gave me a wonderful time. His Australian friends were so hospitable and friendly.

It was a land of milk and honey. The Australians ate like kings, huge steaks, thick meaty fish. The seafood was superb. No wonder Pat had put on so much weight.

It was a happy, euphoric interlude. I have never laughed, ate and drunk so much in all my life. One day I heard myself laughing at something and it sounded like a creaky, rusty engine. It was only then, I realised, that I had not laughed in a long time. It was magic.

I travelled at speed on a motor launch on the beautiful Swan River sipping champagne and orange juice and eating chicken. I went horse riding in the Bush and played cricket in the sunshine on Christmas Day. All around me there seemed to be happy smiling faces. A sunny climate and a little more affluence seemed to make all the difference.

I even found a charming, corrugated iron Spiritualist Church in Subiaco in the suburbs.

My brother and his wife worked during the day so I developed the habit of sunbathing in the mornings before midday and in the afternoons I meditated in the silence in the cool, air-conditioned lounge. These sittings grew into a wonderful daily communication between myself and the friend who had died from cancer not too long before. I have no wish to relate the content of these daily happenings. It was personal and of no interest to anyone else. For a while whilst I was there the contact was strong.

It was with regret that I left my brother and new friends after a few happy months but I was missing my children by that time. They were living their own lives but I didn't like to be away from them for too long. I had a grandchild too by that time

North Wales was grey and cold that winter but it was good to see the girls again. There was no work available in the area at all. Some friends from London suggested that I stay with them whilst I tried to find work there. It was hopeless. I tried to get a job and tramped the streets trying to find a flat but without suitable employment I couldn't hope to make a home. My suntan soon faded along with any feeling of well being.

After a month of this without any luck I returned to Wales where I knew that once the season started I would find something. The only highlight of the month had been the occasional visit to the S N U HQ in Belgrave Square where I met a Medium that I had previously encountered at the College of Psychic Studies in Essex. I attended some of her classes.

She was good, she did sand readings and was an excellent reacher. I thoroughly enjoyed the sessions with her I remember that she told me that I was being stripped bare, that I was being tested and to imagine myself as being like a tree being savagely exposed without any foliage

29

at all and then the buds would bloom and blossom and grow into a thing of beauty. Very poetic and not very comforting at the time I must admit.

In Wales I set up home again and with the remainder of my money I bought furnishings and a little Citroen Dyane car. I worked for the season and was quite comfortable.

Winter came again and the work finished, so, still interested in Psychic Research I did a little Healing with a gifted friend, Helen. We would visit people in their homes who needed help. Clairvoyantly I did occasional Psychometry readings when asked. To do this one holds an object, usually metal, in your hands and give out your impressions as you stroke the object and concentrate. People seemed pleased and very often would tell me that the things that I had told them had come true.

At that time every time that I heard a news bulletin about one atrocity or another in Northern Ireland I would get very distressed, and mentally I was always saying "Please God, can't you do something about Northern Ireland?"

One night I was disturbed from my sleep seemingly by someone who was trying to communicate mentally with me. At that time in my life I was very involved in Psychic work and had many friends in that field. The communication was quite strong.

It was a young Irishman who said his name was Dermot O'Reilly. I can only imagine that he was drawn to me because of my distress at the carnage that seemed to be happening daily. He urged me to help. I did write down what he was saying. Long patriotic speeches about how the violence must be stopped and how he was once a violent man but now he realised how wrong he had been.

I did send his words to a National Newspaper and generally showed the articles around but in actual fact there was little that I could do. People said that the episode was interesting. Although I sympathised and longed to help in some way the mysterious young man who invaded my thoughts so regularly, I could not see how. Eventually this contact stopped. The sadness however at the merciless horror of Irish terrorism lodged deep into my psyche.

Childhood memories of the bitterness and the hypocrisy and intolerance of sectarianism was always with me. If I could have harnessed and utilised any psychic wisdom and power to try to stop these events, I would have done, but I did not have the knowledge or the experience to try. Every time a violent incident occurred my frustration grew at not being able to do a thing about it.

For the next few years I carried on working only in the summer months. In the winter I was poverty stricken and devoted the empty months to my interest, Psychic Research.

Some of the Psychics that I came across seemed quite good but also there were the ones who were bizarre and frankly ridiculous. I do not suffer fools gladly and longed for intelligent sources to help me to advance myself psychically.

I had a gifted friend, Helen, whom I often accompanied on her visits to a young woman who suffered from MS and had severe throat problems. We called on Judy to give her Healing, Spiritual Healing. In her early thirties, Judy was very ill indeed. Our visits seemed to bring her comfort. the very first moment that I touched her I had a vivid mental picture of her mother, whom she lived with, dressed all in black. There was no way that Helen and I could help Judy to become well again. She was always glad to see us though and for a little while afterwards would feel stronger.

One evening I was sitting quietly in my home when I 'sensed' a man with me. He explained that he was Judy's father and he asked me to tell her that he was looking after her. I was reluctant to do this as I was afraid that it would alarm her and that she would think that she was going to die. I did tell her, however, rather hesitantly. For a moment she seemed to regret that her father could see her in such a poor state. Then she seemed to gain strength and talked much about him.

Judy seemed to be fading fast however and when I was with her all I seemed to sense was daffodils. I thought that a change would come when the daffodils bloomed and promised her that I would take her outside to see them in the Springtime. Helen and I planned to wheel her outside in her wheelchair. About six weeks later I received a phone call to say that Judy had died. I just felt so relieved that for Judy the suffering was over.

31

On the way to the funeral, in Helen's car, everywhere we looked daffodils were growing in profusion. It was a golden sunny day with a warm Spring breeze. It was made all the more golden by the beautiful yellow blooms.

During the service I nudged Helen and asked if she could see anything. She shook her head at me. To my surprise and delight, I could see everything. Judy was in the church with her father. She looked beautiful, healthy and glowing. She wore a white dress with pink roses on it and she walked around the church looking curiously into the pews to see who had come to her service. She held a bunch of daffodils out to me smiling. It was not a sad occasion for me, quite the opposite.

When I told her later, Judy's mother was comforted to know that her daughter had been there in the church.

I felt honoured to have witnessed such a sad yet happy event and was truly grateful that I had been allowed to see it.

At around this time I met a man at my place of work. I was still very lonely and longed for a male partner but never seemed to meet anyone.

I was introduced to this man and on shaking hands with him I was immediately repelled by him. I shivered and couldn't take my hand away quickly enough. I avoided him, not liking my first impressions.

It was on a visit to London to an appointment in Belgrave Square, on realising that I was too early I went into the nearby Plumbers Arms to kill some time.To my surprise I found this man standing next to me at the bar. Both a bit staggered about meeting hundreds of miles from home he urged me to come back after my appointment to have a drink with him. We had a friendly chat and he was very witty and entertaining so I agreed.

I had second thoughts afterwards. I got tied up with interesting Psychic people and did not turn up as promised. Then I promptly forgot all about him.

Months later we did meet again at work and he seemed to be a very funny man. He made me laugh so much. He was quite a comedian, so I was drawn into friendship with him. He was a generous and attentive man who made me feel attractive and for a change everything seemed to go so well. We became inseparable and my loneliness vanished. Eventually I moved in with him full of hope for a happier future.

Any misgivings that I may have had about him during those first months I pushed to the back of my mind. Women always think that they can change a man and if at times he seemed to be a bit secretive about where he had been and what he had been doing I did not worry too much.

Gradually however a dark side to his personality emerged and he proved to be a real Jekyll and Hyde character. I struggled for a while hoping that things would change but it was a forlorn hope. I packed my bags and left him.

I had chosen to ignore my first impressions. I was repelled by his handshake on that first meeting and had gone ahead anyway and formed an attachment to him. In a way I suppose it was my own fault. I should have trusted my instincts which in the end had proved to be right.

Again with hindsight when I look back there is much that I have to thank him for. He gave me more confidence in myself and there had been many good moments but as a permanent long-term relationship it was very ill starred.

I went off in my little car to East Sussex and miserable and lonely, even at times contemplating walking into the sea. I found a job in a hotel as a Silver Service waitress.

Upstairs in the hotel the decor was lovely but downstairs in the staff accommodation it was a different story. It was tatty and infested with cockroaches, but it was a relief to have a job and a bed. All the other waiters and waitresses were very young. We worked three shifts a day six days a week and sometimes I was very tired. Their cheerful casualness however was very infectious and they treated me like one of themselves, which was very nice.

I did a few Psychic readings for them for fun and once even did a reading for a millionaire guest in the hotel. He took me and a couple of the young girl waitresses for a ride in his Rolls Royce and then he took us all to dinner. It was lovely. We laughed so much. They were such lovely company for me at that time.

In one of the hotels a Psychic Society held weekly meetings. I joined and met many interesting people. There was a husband and wife team whom I liked very much. He had a surgery in town to do reflexology. In my off-duty hours I went along and talked for hours to him about his work. As well as treating his patients by manipulating their feet, he was clairvoyant and used to give them sound advice as well. I was fascinated.

They had a lovely home just outside the seaside town in the country. They had numerous animals and the lady looked after most of them. They ran a Healing Sanctuary for sick and wounded animals. It was a friendly, informal place with horses grazing outside the large, welcoming, cluttered kitchen. They held regular gatherings in their home. Interesting people were invited to lecture on various subject. Colour Healing, Meditation, The Tarot, Trees, Yoga, Precious Stones. There were musical evenings and I must admit that I enjoyed this Bohemian company.

Max and Nancy said that they drew their energy from their beautiful pastoral home surroundings, even from the animals themselves. I could well believe it. It was a very instructive and fascinating period for me, attending these gatherings. Privately I wondered sometimes if some of the lecturers were a little bit 'batty' but they were all very nice.

I had a strange experience in the cinema one day. I was watching the film "Ghandi" alone on a night off. A voice in my head told me that one day I would work in Ireland. It was a male voice and very clear. I did not see how that could come about as I have no contacts in Ireland and although my roots were there had no family there at all. It seemed very unlikely even though I was deeply concerned about the bad reports continually being broadcast about Irish affairs. I continued to watch the film about India perhaps making slight comparisons to my own situation.

The season drew to a close in East Sussex and although sadness had brought me there after a broken relationship, I had enjoyed and learned much from my interesting friends.

Once again I went back north on my own without a male partner. I seemed fated not to have a successful relationship so thought that maybe it would be better to live alone without any emotional trauma but I must admit it took years to find a serenity that can only come through being alone. I gained a peace and became more self-sufficient through all my struggles and hardships.

My two daughters and grandchildren brought tremendous happiness in my life. I had much to be grateful for. My trips home to Widnes were always frequent to my mother and family. I could never be away from them for too long. 'Stinky' Widnes was always at the centre of my wanderings.

I attended many seminars at that time and listened to many good lecturers and demonstrators. One whom I particularly admired, could give much accurate information - names, addresses and even car registration numbers. Sometimes the demonstrations were not always so good. It varied.

I suspect myself that like a radio receiver, sometimes the communication was patchy and unclear. It must be awful to be on a platform demonstrating and your source dries up. I think that this happens often. Then, I am sure, some people try to bluff their way through. One can hardly dry up standing in front of a room full of people. It is my opinion that even the best then resort to trying to cheat, even though they may be brilliant most of the time.

That is why at times there are stories of deception but for me it does not damage the credibility of the powers of the Psychic who generally performs well. The pressure to produce evidence is tremendous and I am sure that very often all that they can get is a blank. Then the imagination takes over or even bluff. It is not possible to perform brilliantly all the time.

It was at about this time that I had another unusual experience.

Although over the years I had many familiar clairvoyant episodes, two experiences were startling in their clarity and in the fact that I was wide awake but relaxed when they occurred. I was in my home calmly surveying the room when suddenly the room vanished! In its place, like a huge technicoloured screen, was the sky. Across the brilliant blue sky an aeroplane sped quickly across. I saw a group of Arabs on a hillside gesticulating and shouting as the aeroplane dropped missiles and two huge mushroom clouds filled the sky.

It was so vivid, so real!

I knew with certainty that this was something almost superhuman that had occurred and it must be very important. What it meant, however, I didn't know. No words of explanation were spoken this time and the vision faded leaving me puzzled and confused but sure that at some time in the future I would understand it all.

When the second Super Vision came I still had not found an explanation for the first one.

I was again awake but relaxed in a different home some two to three years later. I remember that it was November and grey and cold.

Again the room vanished.

This time I was standing in a beautiful lush green field. The birdsong, every blade of grass was accentuated vividly. It was accompanied by a feeling of euphoria and delight as I watched a group of chestnut brown horses as they nudged each other playfully and gambolled in warm sunshine. It was a wonderful sight and I felt such pleasure as I witnessed the scene. In the distance I saw the back of what appeared to be a brown robed monk. Unnaturally and at speed I was drawn across the field. I did not walk. The monk turned towards me. Where his face should have been, underneath the cowled headgear, all I could see was a swathe of bandages. The hood fell down revealing the head which was indeed swathed in bandages. At high speed a layer unravelled and underneath each layer there seemed to be another layer. As this was happening, thoughts, feelings and words tumbled through my mind which turned out later to be my life's future events played rather like a fast forward on a radio cassette. Finally the last layer unravelled and underneath was the face of corruption, full of sores. It was horrible. The eyes were bright though and clear blue. As I watched the face changed and became beautiful.

As these strange things were happening to me a voice spoke to me. It seemed an old, old voice, a little cracked in tone and seemed to come from a distance. The voice said to me:

"You have had to face incredible misfortune. This will now be put right by divine inspiration and your guideline to this will be the American political scene".

Then the whole vision faded and I was in bed again.

Agitated, puzzled and totally without any understanding I was bemused by the whole thing. I rang my eldest daughter to tell her and neither of us could make out what it could mean I never forgot the words however. It was years before I was to understand these experiences.

I had made friends with a group of ladies who were on my wavelength and were very intelligent and we met up weekly for meditation and psychic development.

One evening we were told to read all that we could about the Russian Monk Rasputin who supposedly had incredible powers. I found the story of this man fascinating. As far as I could tell from the books that I read this man had a lovely endearing side to his nature. Unfortunately he fell prey to sexual and alcoholic excesses. Apparently he was unable to overcome his many weaknesses. There was no doubt about it Rasputin had very strong clairvoyant and Healing Powers. If he could only have overcome the baser side of his nature the whole course of Russian history could have been changed.

As I read his story I felt a tremendous sympathy for him. Perhaps because I have fallen for likable rogues in the past to my cost.

I found it sad that he had misused the trust and responsibility of his obvious gifts.

37

Nearer to home, I admired the work of Helen Duncan, a Scottish Medium, who had been sent to jail for betraying Official Secrets even though nobody bothered to find out how she had received the information. 'Battling Bertha' Harris I admired too. She was from Chester, not far from Widnes.

None of our group seemed to move forward much though and I remember reading Shirley McLaine's books and recognising her struggle for Spiritual Awareness. I can remember saying to my friend, Sonia, wistfully envious of Shirley's experiences, "That's what we could do with Sonia, a few mystical experiences in Peru!"

I longed to visit some of these Ancient civilisations to tune in to the almost certainly, wonderful vibrations. A wet and windy day in Colwyn Bay didn't hold the same magic for us somehow!

Sonia worked in a Nursing Home with elderly people and listening to Sonia's tales about her work I thought that at least she was helping people.

At that time it was winter again and I wasn't working.

I did a few readings for people with the Tarot but wasn't happy with it. Sometimes it would flow quite well and others I would struggle. I didn't like taking any money for it and to be honest people came to me so unhappy, trying to get me to tell them that they were going to get married, move house, have an affair, come into money. I felt responsible for them and was unhappy myself if I couldn't tell them what they wanted to hear.

One woman came and it was apparent that she had three men in her life at the same time. She pestered the life out of me. In the end I stopped doing it. I felt that if I had any Powers at all that I would have liked to utilise them to help mankind, not just to be a Fortune Teller.

Some of the tasks that Sonia had to perform for her patients I felt repulsed by. I thought "I can't do that". I had a tremendous respect for her because sometimes she was weary with her efforts.

Then, I don't quite know how it happened, I had been moaning to my family about how fed up I was of doing 'bum' jobs for very little reward.

I found myself working for very low pay in a Nursing Home and I saw more bums in a week than I had in my entire life. I was shattered by what I saw there. Senility, stroke victims, so much helplessness through ill health and old age. It was heartbreaking.

My frustration that I wasn't doing very spiritual work eased then as I clumsily and inexpertly but willingly tried to help. I do not think that I had ever really thought about the problems of old age before. Some of these elderly men and women were entirely reliant on the kindness and care of the staff. I felt that they were souls that had become trapped in bodies that had become a burden to them.

My younger daughter joined me in this work. Like myself she found work hard to find. I would pick her up in my car and we went together. She is a kind, compassionate girl and the old people loved her. She was never afraid of hard work.

For myself there then followed a strange, beautiful period of Psychic development when many times with terminally ill patients I saw dead relatives around the bed as if waiting for their loved ones to join them. Sometimes the patients seemed to see them too. For they spoke to them smiling as if comforted.

A tremendous compassion grew inside me for these elderly people whose quality of life had become very poor. I tried to make the unpleasant, personal tasks become insignificant although I was still a bit queasy and often it was hard.

Some were very demanding and could be very difficult but most of them were very sweet and very grateful for any kindness. Winnie, a particular favourite of my daughter and I, who used to be in the Salvation Army, would look at us both and say "What are you doing here in this place with us old fogeys? You should be out enjoying yourselves!"

Another favourite of mine had been a solicitor and a very intelligent man. Senility had made his body a shuffling burden. He spilled his food, he was incontinent and he was very unhappy. He would sit slumped, deep in his thoughts and sometimes tears would escape from the corners of his eyes. "I feel old" he would reply to my enquiry if he was all right.

He died one day when I was off duty. A few days later when I was tidying up his room he just appeared at the side of me. The old shuffling man in the soiled clothes had gone. He wore a light grey suit with white shirt and bright red tie. He was shining, positively glowing. His hair was still grey but he looked younger, alert and upright. Vividly alive is how best I would have described him. He did not speak. He just smiled as if to say "Look at me now!" It was truly beautiful.

When the sight of him faded away I rushed eagerly to tell some of the other Nurses but I pulled up short when I saw fear in their faces. My daughter was used to me and my sightings but the others were afraid so I learned to keep quiet about most of my experiences. I had no wish to frighten them.

One day when I came on duty Winnie appeared to be a little unwell. We put her to bed and I checked her regularly. She was just 'out of sorts'. She still chattered away and there seemed to be no need for undue alarm. Before going off duty I popped in to see her and was alarmed to hear a terrible noise coming from her throat. I sent for the Matron who quickly assessed the situation. Winnie was dying. She went to telephone the doctor and left me kneeling by her bed. I held her hand and stroked her hair saying aloud "Don't worry Winnie, everything will be all right".

Mentally I asked God and her family to help her. Within seconds it seemed I felt her body temperature go down. She died in my arms. I was amazed that death had come so quickly. With a mixture of relief and sadness for Winnie, I felt then that death was like a butterfly breaking free from a heavy burdensome chrysallis. Winnie was free, she was off somewhere, out of this place that had imprisoned her. What I held in my arms, held nothing of Winnie, it was just an empty shell.

At the time all I was concerned about was helping her and did not experience her soul leaving the body. I did not even try to tune in. So I saw nothing.

It was after the doctor had been and had pronounced her dead that I washed Winnie for the last time. It was the last act of kindness that I could do for her and I was gentle with her as I whispered goodbye to her as I pictured a beautiful butterfly flying free.

I surprised myself. I never thought that I could have performed this task for a person who had died. I was genuinely fond of her.

Things got a little hectic then, a policeman came. It was the procedure with a sudden death. I was sitting in the kitchen telling the policeman exactly what had happened when I heard quite clearly Winnie's voice saying "I don't know what you are all worried about. I'm out of the bloody lot if it now!" I laughed aloud and one of the other nurses looked scared. "You've just seen something, haven't you?" she said. Mentally, I blocked off then. I just shook my head.

My daughter and I went to Winnie's funeral but unlike my experience with Judy, the young MS girl who had died and I had seen at her own funeral, I saw no sign of Winnie. She was so glad to go that she wasn't coming back for anything.

All in all, that period of time was very rewarding. I saw and felt many things but it got to the stage when I was waiting for the next person to die. It was like being in God's waiting room.

I felt that my daughter should be having fun and although we had both learned a deep compassion for others, I felt that it was unhealthy to do this job for too long.

Then I started to work with young people who were 'In Care', some of them being Educationally Sub Normal. They were aged between 16-26 but some of them were little more than children.

I have done many jobs in my life, many which I have loathed, but suddenly I found myself doing one of the most rewarding jobs of work. It was no hardship to get up in the morning to go to work.

To say that these kids were misfits would be an understatement. Many had been abused, sexually and physically by their own families.

Many had lived in the most appaling conditions of deprivation. Nearly all of them had a terrible, smouldering anger and frustration inside themselves.

The Boarding School was situated in the Vale of Clwyd and housed a hundred youngsters. At first I was a little frightened when one of the youngsters would go 'berserk'. It was quite common for them to break

41

windows and hit out at whoever was nearest. It may have been that one of them had just had a disappointment or was upset. They found it hard to express their feelings. Sometimes they injured themselves deliberately. I found it touching when some of the young members of staff calmly soothed the youngster. If they were very violent a young man in charge would push the angry male or female on to the ground and would sit on them, whilst gently coaxing them to say what was wrong. They were treated with such care and compassion by people who were not much older than themselves.

So many of the residents were unloved. They had no-one. Some of their families could not cope with their needs - unwanted, unlovely and unloved. Some were exceptions but their parents could not have them at home for one reason or another.

Slowly, I learned from the other staff to keep discipline but yet to be caring. We had lots of laughs. The humour of the young staff was very infectious and the children were very affectionate.

The rewards were tremendous. I worked in a unit of 24 young male residents. I laughed with them, I cried with them and felt a tremendous love for them growing in me.

I drove a Mini Bus to take them on outings, into the pub, out for a meal, to the seaside. We went for long walks in the leafy lanes around the School. They could be very demanding and all clamouring for attention at the same time. Sometimes I felt tired and drained.

We all ate together and staff did sleep in duties on a rota to be available at night. There was cricket and football in the summer.

I enjoyed the laughter and the camaraderie there and it was good for me to know what it was to look after so many of Nature's imperfections with genuine love and kindness.

One of the boys, I will call him David, could see Spirit People. Sometimes at night he would see members of his family in his room. Usually it was his grandmother. It was the other members of staff who told me this. I personally did not discuss it with him. I was just interested that he could 'see'. From events that happened later I am not surprised that David had seen so much activity.

42

He was a religiously devout boy. He would sit on the stairs and sing hymns in a sweet, sad plaintive voice. He missed his Church and his family. His body was older than his mind and he had frightened a little girl by trying to play games with her quite innocently but it was bizarre for a grown man to act this way. It was a sad story.

He was found dead in the bath by a member of staff one morning. He had not drowned. His head was slumped on his shoulder as if he was asleep. He had just quietly died.

For a few nights afterwards banging noises came from David's room. No-one saw anything but the Night Duty man was puzzled when he could find no explanation.

Mentally, I tried to reach him. I asked him not to frighten the other boys and told him that now he could go; he didn't have to stay here any longer. I didn't 'see' David at all but the banging did stop.

I enjoyed the time that I spent there. The old people and the young ones had made me aware of other people's pain and suffering. I had seen their loneliness, their rejection and their deprivation.

It made me a better human being.

My friend, Sonia, told me of an advertisement that she had seen for an Administrative Assistant at the Psychic College in Essex that I had attended on courses.

Still drawn to this and torn a little because I enjoyed my present work I sent off an application. I got the job. I was interviewed by a committee, one of who was a Psychic that I much admired who was very charming and courteous. He told me that accommodation would be very limited. Outside in the village it would be very expensive if it could be found at all. He said, however, that I could make full use of the education facilities in the College.

He said I was to be given a large room in the Stable Block and there would be a small kitchen with kitchen facilities.

Although my heart plummeted like a stone because the salary was small and I would not have a proper home I accepted because I was keen

43

to learn as much as I could of Psychic Research. The carrot offered was too big to refuse in spite of niggling worries.

I thought that I was on the Yellow Brick Road! How wrong I was!

On my arrival my fears about the accommodation was realised. The large room' turned out to be little more than a cupboard in the stable. The kitchen was a scruffy, bare-boarded room, with a sink unit and cupboard that had doors which would not close. There was no cooker at all. The stable took the overflow from the College which had bedrooms and a few bathrooms. The kitchen was just a place to make tea.

It was late in the evening and I was so tired and dispirited. I unpacked my electric kettle and a few belongings and made coffee. Most of my belongings had to stay in the car.

Next morning I approached the General Manager. I knew from previous experience he could be curt and rude to people. I was working for the Committee not for him but I could not find anyone else. "Oh dear", he said tartly. It was none of his business but if I came back later he would allow me to have a meal in the Dining Room until it was sorted out. So I went back and that one meal lasted me all day.

I wasn't unduly worried at that time as I thought someone would help me. I reported for duty on the Monday and was given an apology over the mix up over kitchen facilities. They told me to go to the Dining Room for meals in the meantime. This was fine until the Saturday. I sat in the Dining Room amongst new arrivals for that week's course when the Manager spotted me. He must not have noticed me all week. He was horrified. He threw his hands in the air and told me in front of everyone that it was not his responsibility to feed me and turned me away red faced and embarrassed which I felt was very cruel.

I found a shop open in the village and lived on bread and cold meat for three days as it was a Bank Holiday weekend.

I had been made as welcome as the flowers in May!

There was a lot of infighting among the management of the College at that time and I only found out some years later that there had been a serious rift between the College organisers and serious accusations had been made. I knew none of this at the time though and thought everyone unfriendly and unhelpful. None of it was personal at all. There was just a lot of trouble going on underneath the surface.

Educationally speaking it was food and drink to me. I listened to everything that was said. I didn't always agree with everything but it was wonderful. I was amongst people on my own wavelength. I made many friends amongst the guests who came from all over the world to attend courses. As the guests changed weekly it was not possible to join a steady regular group for development so I travelled into the College of Psychic Studies in South Kensington one night a week with a talented group.

A small Belling cooker was bought for the inadequate kitchen but really facilities were very bad. I came across an advertisement for a cottage in return for housework and babysitting. The College agreed to share me so I did both jobs and moved into the cottage relieved to have a decent place to stay.

My other employer was a rich gentleman farmer's wife. With hindsight it seemed that I had made an error of judgement. Oh, did she want her pound of flesh. It was a disaster. In trying to please both of them I found it increasingly difficult to get into Kensington one precious night a week. A few times I arrived late and could not get in because once the session had started the door could not be opened. One evening I saw my face in the Tube window and I looked like 'death warmed up' but I struggled on because I was doing what I enjoyed. My abilities were strengthening and at times as I walked around amongst the trees in the beautiful grounds I seemed to crackle like an electric light bulb. There was so much energy in the College and grounds. At times I felt intoxicated even though I hadn't been drinking. It was a magical, unearthly feeling. I felt at one with nature.

So I carried on, although at times I was envious of the rich lady as I made her beds and cleaned her house whilst she played tennis outside with her chums. Their laughter drifted up to me. The children of the house had everything that they could possibly want and I thought of the 'poor buggers' that I had left behind in Wales. Although it was a struggle I felt that it was worth it, until one night, after doing far too much, I haemorrhaged very badly alone in the cottage. I nearly dialled 999 but I survived the night and managed.

There was still a lot of tension in the College, with inside jealousies and conflict and the more it went on the more I became disappointed. My health did not improve. So get away from all the bitterness and feeling that I had failed miserably and lost out on such a golden opportunity, I returned to North Wales. I felt if I was going to be ill that I wanted to be near my family. Sick with disappointment I turned my back on the paranormal for two years.

I returned to my old job back at the school in Wales. Everyone welcomed me back with open arms, both youngsters and staff. It was lovely to be amongst friends.

I rented a tiny house from a friend of my daughters and was happy enough although I did not have much money with running a home, as I was again not well paid. My health was not brilliant and I had to see a specialist as at times I had colossal haemorrhages. If I had a prescription with more than one item it was difficult to scrape by financially. That is why when I saw an advertisement for a rent and rate free cottage in return for minimum caretaking duties I went for it, providing it was minimum, as I had to work at the school as well.

I got an interview and as I drove to the address about 20 minutes drive away from the school I found that it was a castle. It stood high in the hills overlooking the valley and had the most breathtaking panoramic views.

As I drove up the long drive it was like a fairytale. It was spring and the fields were ablaze with multitudes of golden daffodils swaying in the breeze. Not quite able to believe it I drove up to the front door. It turned out to be a rich man's folly. A modern castle built with local stone by local tradesmen.

The owners were only there at weekends as they lived in London and it transpired that they wanted very little in the way of work. They had been burgled so really they just wanted someone to be there and to switch the heating on when they were due to arrive from London.

The cottage was in the castle compound and was beautifully decorated with large rooms and with a wood burning stove in the massive lounge. It was all very luxurious. I had to pinch myself to make sure that it was real when they picked me for the job out of many others that they had seen. It couldn't have been more different than the squalid surroundings of the Psychic College. So now, with not having to pay any rent I was living a more affluent life. The place was a dream. My feet didn't touch the floor for ages.

My health improved a little in this picturesque place. There was only myself and the sheep that grazed on the hillsides. I felt like Bo-Peep.

My daughters and grandchildren came over to stay many times and so did my family from Widnes. We walked and went to the nearest Pub for lunches. I sat in the sun amongst all the luxury, revelling in the warmth on my face and remembered when I was a young teenager and sat sunbathing in the backyard, next to the dustbin in Caroline Street. The sun then had to struggle through the fumes and smoke of industrial Widnes. This place was a long way from Caroline Street. Like going from rags to riches I thought happily as I remembered my Dad and hundreds like him clattering down the cobbles of the back alley in his dust coated clogs and flat cap. He never got the chance to see anything of the world, I thought sadly.

I brought some of the boys up regularly from the School in the Mini Bus and they would cart logs from the wood shed up to the castle for me. It was an idyllic interlude.

I thought little of the paranormal and my disappointment at my last venture, although occasionally, when there was a news bulletin about yet another sectarian murder in Northern Ireland I wished that there was something that I could do about it. Whilst I was at the College, my idea had been to get the best help to develop into a good Psychic and maybe to utilise it in some way to go to Ireland as I knew some of them did go to Belfast with their work. It hadn't come off, so there was no point in dwelling on it. I wasn't prepared to struggle again in that way.

At Christmas the owners had a massive firework display and my cottage was full with relatives enjoying themselves. We did have snow that winter and sometimes it was difficult to get to work. My car broke down at one stage and I could not get to work at all. I had to take leave. One winter night the alarms went off outside the castle walls. If anyone came up the drive at night an alarm would ring as a warning. I couldn't see anything but nervous I rang for the Police who couldn't see anything either although they searched the grounds. This happened a few times and I must admit that it began to make me feel a bit vulnerable especially as the castle had recently been featured in a Magazine. A woman lone in the dark winter nights could very well be an easy target for the unscrupulous.

I read a lot, as always, and one cold winter night I read a book by Jennie Lee on Aneurin Bevan, "My Life with Nye". I don't know why, but as I read this book about this man and his extraordinary determination, in spite of opposition and at times hatred and spite, an overwhelming urge came over me that I had not got to shut myself away, luxurious as it was in my surroundings, but I had to get out and find what it was that would lead me to my own destiny.

After another suspected intruder, I decided I would leave the Castle and a strange chain of events led me back to Widnes where I stayed with one of my sisters whilst I worked out what to do. I found a part-time office job which kept the wolf from the door and I scanned the papers and the Job Centres for work.

After two years of turning my back on the Paranormal world I decided to visit once again a Spiritualist Church in Widnes. When we were growing up, my sisters and I had avoided this Church like the plague. In the area that I lived, it had sinister connections, so it was strange that I should be sitting there.

The demonstrator, a young man, gave me a message. He said that I would go to London and that I would talk to a man in a uniform. I just said "Oh". I couldn't imagine myself down south again. I was enjoying being back in Widnes in the bosom of my family again.

My early childhood years featured prominently in my mind. My grandmother, Mary Jane McCarthy, and my Aunt Molly singing Irish songs in their beautiful singing voices during regular sing-songs. The laughter and the Irish flavour of our lives came back and although the houses had been demolished in Newtown now, I walked where they had once been. I recaptured the essence of what we all were - myself, my sisters, brothers and Mam. The feelings were very strong and very beautiful. All the laughter and all the pathos of those days. The strong family ties. The neighbours and the smell and sound of Caroline Street. I recalled all the children from the different families, their lives so intertwined. A conglomeration of people from Catherine Street, Victoria Street, Margaret Street, Charlotte Street, George Street, Elizabeth Street. The Pubs on every corner.

In my mind's eye I walked down these streets again as they once were, saw faces that I knew standing in their doorways. The women in their pinnies, the men in their clogs coming home from work, mutton cloth scarves wound around their necks and flat caps on their heads. I saw hordes of children playing street games - Lallio, Tin Can, Skipping, Two Ball, Alleys, Tops & Whips and Wooden Soap Boxes with wheels.

I saw children pushing prams with their younger brothers and sisters in their charge. Our Patrick and Edward with the backsides out of their trousers and black rings around their legs where their wellies had been. Our Ann, rosy cheeked with a mop of wiry, curly hair. 'Pansy Potter' the other kids called her. She hated that! Our Nora, bespectacled and giggling, Christine who was a beautiful baby and Marie Julie who was always crying.

I remembered being a pupil in St Maries School, so strictly Victorian and unyielding. The female teachers stern and full if discipline. The Church where I knelt runny nosed in the pews - my nose always ran in Church.

As I stood in that empty space that had once housed so many people I marvelled at all the activity and raw human life that had once occurred there. Now it seemed such a small area for so many people to have lived out the drama of their lives. The very air seemed highly charged with past events.

Still left standing on the corner a grimy solitary tribute to the past was Redmonds Pub. How often I had lain in bed sleepily, listening as the noisy revellers made their way home to the sound of singing or arguing or fighting and window smashing as noisy disagreements ensued, sometimes between husband and wife.

I include here a not very good poem that I wrote years ago. The metre is questionable but the feeling is there.

CAROLINE STREET

The clatter of clogs
On a cobbled yard
The faces of women
Impassive and hard.
A baby straddles
On her ample hip
As she stands in her doorway
To chatter and gossip.

Saturday night Grandad
Locks Nanny out
As she comes home singing
With two bottles of stout.
She bangs and shouts and
Makes such a din
Finally, Grandad
He lets her come in.

They scutter and
Grandad starts to shout
Nanny, she gets the
Insurance policies out.
"I'll outlast you, you bugger
You'll go before I do!"
He did go first and
She spent it all too.

Mam at the washtub
With her 'dolly blue'
Newspaper tablecloths
And dumplings and stew.
Water running in
A constant stream
No time for Mam
To sit and dream.

Hairy string skipping ropes
And comics to swop.
Sticks of wood liquorice
From Cassidy's shop.
Hot summer pavements, somersaults
With bare legs up the wall
Hopscotch and spinning tops
And games of 'Two Ball'.

A snowy white dress
In the May procession.
More brothers and sisters
In a rapid succession.
'The Catholic Times'
On the sideboard to see
The 'News of the World'
Hidden down the settee.

Mam, Nora and myself in
Caroline St.

Mam's sister Molly,
Green eyes and dark hair
After her many eyes turned
Around just to stare.
Young as I was, I think
I knew then
She could make little dwarfs
Out of very big men!

Mam's brother Paddy
Bursts into song
He was always right
He was never wrong.
Home from the Army
To tell a fine tale
I sit on his knee
As he sups up his ale.

51

Mam, Molly, Nanny
Our Paddy and me
We chatter and chaff
While I mash the tea.
Paddy picks Nanny up
To his strong, young chest.
Out of all of her children
Nanny loves him the best.

He rubs at her face
With his dark, bristly chin.
My Nanny's face softens
As she looks up at him.
She pretends she is cross
She gives him a slap!
He hits her back
With a sweet, loving tap.

Tommy Connor's Saloon Bar
And the beery breath
From chemical filled lungs
Which caused many a death.
Rich only in laughter
In surroundings so grim
With an unquenchable spirit
That no sadness could dim.

Mam's pain as Dad's
Coffin is laid in the ground
The grief on her face
So pretty and round
"My God", she cries
"What will I do?"
My little brother Edward
"Mam I'll look after you!"

Christmas with books
Many pages unread.
A cold winters night
With three warm in a bed.
Chips with brown sauce
Stew with rubber meat
Mam working so hard
To give us a treat.

How far I am now
From Caroline Street
Nanny and Molly are
Not there to greet.
But I remember their spirit
Their beauty, their strife,
I will love and remember
For the rest of my life.

As I stood years later on that waste ground I felt as if I had come on a pilgrimage. My sisters and I went for a drink to Redmonds Pub. There were people in there who we knew. They still travelled back long distances to drink there. As we drank and talked I sensed many unseen visitors in the background. Long gone now but the vibrations were still there. It was sad.

My family did not share my interest in Psychic affairs but i did get them to go along one evening with me to a Service. As we were singing a hymn I noticed that my sister Julie's shoulders were shaking with mirth. I thought "Oh no, we are going to get thrown out in a minute!" I looked at her questioningly and she pointed hysterically at the Medium's feet. The elderly lady was dressed in a blue Crimplene dress, pink woolly cardigan, thick support tights and the most luridly coloured training shoes that I had ever seen in my life. She sang heartily in full flow "All things bright and beautiful". It was hard to take anything seriously after that. I have found the frankly bizarre and the ridiculous in some of the Churches but I am convinced, that at the core of all this eccentricity, I have found the Truth. All the rest is just sheer entertainment

In my searching amongst advertisements for a job after sending off dozens of applications I came across one that read:

Are you tired of boring mundane jobs? Why not try working for services welfare with the British Army? Aged over 35 years with experience in community and welfare work.

Just joking to my family really I said "I'm going to join the Army!" As I sat on the train from Runcorn going down to London for interview with an Army Major. I remembered just a few weeks before being told that I was going to London to talk to a man in uniform. Somehow I knew that this job had my name on it. Maybe it would take me to Northern Ireland. It did! Interviews had taken place in Brixton in London and I was placed in a group of six women who had been chosen to attend a training session prior to being placed in units throughout the country.

I've never had such fun. We were all fitted out in green uniform in most of which we looked ridiculous. We all looked like demented District Nurses! We stayed at the Union Jack Club and were briefed daily on the Structure of the Army. Rank etc and the Battalions, Regiments, Companies and so on by a serving Colonel in the British Army. Our duties were outlined to us and it all sounded very exciting and at dinner in the evening we all got to know each other as we drank wine, eager to begin this exciting new job. At the end of the Course we were all sad to say goodbye to each other as we separated to go to different Regiments.

I had been sent to the Royal Engineers in Kent. Ann, a lively chatty lady whom I had got on with very well, was sent to Mill Hill, not too far away, so we planned to meet.

I arrived at the Barracks in the late afternoon after the long drive from the north and on arriving at the Officers Mess, which is where I would be living, I was given the key to my room and was waved in the appropriate direction as they were very busy that day as they had a Regimental Dinner on in the evening and I was to attend.

I hauled my bags along the corridor peering sightlessly without my glasses at the nameplates on the door. I reached a door that I thought was mine when I saw that the name actually read K ADIE. I thought "No, someone must be playing a joke". Kate Adie it was. She was one of the guests of honour at the Regimental Dinner. My room was next door.

I spent the evening, totally outshone by Kate Adie, in her little black number and me in my Evans Outsize, hastily bought for the occasion. The skirt was of a satiny material and my table napkin kept sliding off it on to the floor and I am sure the Hooray Henry on my left kept wondering what I was doing with my feet, as I kept trying to pick the dratted thing up between my Freeman & Hardy new shoes and my hand surreptitiously groping down to my raised feet. He made polite conversation all evening but with his plummy accent and the fact that a military band was playing 'The Galloping Major' all through the meal, I couldn't understand a word that he was saying. I just kept nodding and smiling and saying "Oh, really". For his part he must have wondered just who this grinning cretin with St Vitus Dance really was.

Kate had nothing to worry about that night. Although I was the only woman in the room, apart from her, I was no competition. The Officers were all around her afterwards like bees around a honeypot.

The array of silver and crystal on the table was awe inspiring, unlike the asbestos factory that I had once worked in, where they had refused to give us cutlery. There was more silver cutlery than I knew what to do with, because there were six courses. As well as having St Vitus Dance I think that they must have thought that my eyes were crossed because I kept looking at others to see which knife and fork they were using. Oh, yes, Kate definitely had nothing to worry about!

Of course later on I got to enjoy these occasions as I got to know everybody and found these officers to be a light-hearted, happy-go-lucky lot, and the repartee and good humour I shared with them really changed my life. I was having a wonderful time. The NAAFI girls were a grand lot too and included me in a lot of their activities, so for the first time in a long time I was not lonely.

One could not escape the seriousness of Security however as the Deal bombing had just happened. As I watched film of the carnage caused through Irish terrorism it chilled me to the bone at the deadliness of it. I felt for the mothers of the boys who patrolled the streets and who manned the checkpoints. I watched and listened and was overcome by the futility of it. The danger was there all the time. Realistically I wondered what I myself could hope to do but I hadn't got this far without at least trying to play a small part.

I was in Kent for a year and the most dangerous thing that I was involved in was trying to break up a fight between the Paras and the Engineers at the weekly "Stomp", a disco to which local girls were admitted. These stomps were legendary throughout the Army. Just let's say that a nun would have been no good doing my job - she would have been corrupted in no time. It gave me a good grounding however into the Army system.

I heard I was to go to Ireland just as the first of my visions became clear to me, when I saw the exact scene on TV in the Gulf War Report.

I was posted to Northern ireland and on the morning I was to leave Widnes by train I switched on the TV News. A massive bomb had gone off in Londonderry killing five of the soldiers from the very Regiment that I was to be working with, the Kings Regiment. One of the soldiers was from Widnes and was a friend of my niece. All the lads were recruited from the Merseyside area. When I arrived in Ballykelly one of the first squaddies I saw I had known since he was a little boy as I knew his mother. To me this was entirely personal. Most of these lads were of Irish descent.

I could no longer complain that I wasn't doing anything. I was thrown in at the deep end. Hospital visits to the injured soldiers, sympathising and supporting parents, doing all that I could to help, along with the Padre, for the Regiment was shattered by the horrific deaths. I and my colleagues were in the unique position over there of having access to soldiers even at all the deployments. I was even allowed to go into Crumlin Road Jail to visit imprisoned squaddies.

At last I felt I was doing something, if not psychically at least practically, which was far more important at the time. The Regiment got to know me and to trust me and asked me to meet the parents of the dead soldiers who were coming over by plane. I was 'gutted' at their devastation and could see no end to the carnage. It was not all doom and gloom, however, we still had a good time in the Mess. On a 'Greek Night' there was a bit of trouble because everyone went a bit far and broke all the plates in their exuberance.

Over the next months I fell in love with Ireland as I roamed the North Antrim coast, sometimes alone and sometimes with colleagues. Ann from Mill Hill had joined me at this time. The Emerald Isle it certainly was. I have never seen such beauty especially from the air where the greenness is apparent. I have never seen anything like it. A favourite place was the Headland at Port Rush and I can remember being staggered by a field of wild crocuses that I stumbled across in the Spring. The field was thick with the delicately coloured blooms so awe inspiring on a warm sun filled day. It was hard to imagine that so much blood had soaked a land that produced such beauty.

Clairvoyantly I did receive bits and pieces. I knew that my friend Ann's Regiment was going to experience an incident similar to mine but I could not get a time nor a place. I just knew that they were her 'boys'. It did happen but there was nothing that I could do to stop it as it was not enough. I kept receiving the place name Pontefract and later IRA men were apprehended there, but again I could not have been of use. It was as if I was 'blocked' mentally. All I kept being told mentally was that something was going to happen involving children and it would be after that, that people would start to change. I could get no further with that although I strained to try to be able to save life by being alerted to the dangers that may occur. It was not to be.

I would call occasionally in St Finlaughs Church, a picturesque little building on top of the hill outside Ballykelly. It was always when the Church was empty and I would say a silent prayer in there for peace. I loved this Church. It had a simplicity with a tranquil atmosphere and the very fact that it was unadorned and not filled with ornate religious statues and regalia appealed to me. Its simplicity was somehow Holy.

The Colonel allowed me to live out and I lived at the bottom of the hill near the Church in a row of Irish cottages. I got to know my neighbours very well and Michael, a wonderful man, a credit to his race, so kind and helpful and generous. He informed me that he had made the brass cross in the Church with his own hands. It seemed appropriate somehow for a man who had dug his friends out of the rubble of the Drop Inn Well bombing some years previous. The village still reeled from that shock.

So in living in the village I got to the heart of people's feelings about the troubles and I found that the Protestant unionists were more British than the British themselves. Portraits of the Queen received the same reverence that the Pope did amongst Catholics. But by no means did all Catholics want a united Ireland either. Some of them thought that it was financially better to be included in the six counties of Ulster.

There was in all of them though a FEAR! Fear because they did not know who their enemy was. They were careful what they said in public places not knowing who may hear but I am sure that in some way they were anaesthetised against a lot of it. I am sure that they put barriers down when the violence became too much to bear. For them it had gone on for so long in this terrible stalemate fashion.

My daughters and grandchildren came over to stay with me for a holiday but I must admit when they were with me I was afraid for them. Afraid that a bomb may be put under my car whilst they were with me. It was all so unpredictable. My children had not been touched by any personal involvement in Irish affairs. I had given them a life away from any residue of my own Irish upbringing. So I felt it unfair to subject them to any possible violence. So I knew that I would never choose to live permanently in Northern Ireland and I was relieved when they went home.

Although my psychic abilities only produced interesting snippets of actual events, one very interesting thing did happen. I had some visitors to my house one evening - a soldier's wife and her mother who was a Psychic. She would insist that there was something in my hallway. A cold spot she said. "Are you sure" she said,"that there is no unusual activity in this house?" By that she meant Paranormal activity of course. I denied it definitely, saying that I would know about it if there was. I thought that it was her imagination to tell the truth. Either that or that she wasn't a very good Psychic and was exaggerating. I just forgot about it.

My colleagues and I were a good social crowd and we met up often to go out to dinner and even stayed over regularly in each other's homes. We all enjoyed a good laugh and there was a great camaraderie between us. Just one lady seemed a bit quiet and unhappy.

I was travelling back to England by plane one day and we sat next to each other. Something about her was bothering me. "Who's Richard?" I asked. "My husband" she replied quietly. I shut up like a clam then. I knew that her husband was dead but I knew nothing else about her really. I didn't want to upset her.

Back at the house in Ireland again after the visit home I began to be bombarded with impressions and thoughts from this Richard. My house was involved with a strange smell. It was more noticeable in the hallway.

Sometimes a smell denotes a presence rather than an actual sighting. I was convinced that it was Richard and this was confirmed when I sat quietly. He was very concerned for his wife. It had been a terrible tragedy and I have no wish to divulge her personal story but he wanted me to help his wife. I did. I contacted her and she became a regular visitor to my home. It was wonderful to see her smile and join in with the gang on our outings. She became a changed person.

One night when she was staying with me, she and my friend Ann went to bed before I did and as I opened the hall door to go upstairs I nearly gagged the smell was so strong, the air permeated with it. He was definitely there then. I remembered then of course what the lady had said some months before about there being something in the house especially the hallway. She was right in the end. It faded in the end of course, at first becoming hardly noticeable and then when my friend seemed well and happy it just simply disappeared.

I continued to be told every time that I reached out mentally that something would happen involving children and it would be after that that people would change because there would be a massive outcry against it. I could get no clear clairvoyant picture that would have avoided any loss of life no matter how hard I tried, much to my frustration as atrocity after atrocity occurred. It was no use. I had to be content with giving practical help.

It came to the attention of a few people that I was interested in Psychic Research and a Colonel told me of an experience that he had in Hong Kong when he said that he saw a "ghost" - his words. So he was very interested in listening to me. Later on I had occasion to chat with a Cabinet Minister and he told me of a strange experience that his father had. He was sitting in his home when suddenly he saw the figure of his great and good friend standing beside him. The man said "Robert, I have just come to say goodbye!" He found out later of course that his friend was dead. There must be similar stories in every family. Too many stories to discount as nonsense.

My colleagues and I had the honour of being presented with a Military Medal by the Queen Mother and of course we were very proud but I think that the incident that pleased me the most was at a Corporal's Mess Ball when the Colonel of the Regiment asked me to go up on stage to pull a raffle ticket out of a tub for a prizewinner. The cheers and claps raised the roof and the Colonel said to me "See how they love you". That meant more to me than anything. "Everyone knows Mary" the Colonel would say proudly. I loved them too.

Of course all things come to an end and my two years service in Northern ireland was soon up. I despaired that things would never change. Atrocities went on and on. I was posted back to England to a Training Depot to work with Army recruits. I enjoyed very much being in the Cambridge area, and loved the bustle of the river with the punts and the throngs of people and the hundreds of bicycles. It was very pleasant.

The Orchard Tea Gardens with its orchard full of abundant fruit trees and quaint Rupert Brooke ambiance was hard to beat on a sunny day. I drove into Norfolk and to Suffolk and into Linconshire exploring new territory. It was a good opportunity to see parts of England that I had never seen before.

I managed to get home to Widnes fairly frequently and I remember one Spring morning shopping in Warrington with my sister Julie. it was a beautiful day and as I shopped I had no inkling that one week later, in that same place, that a bomb would go off devastating the whole town and surrounding area.

The very next Saturday, when I heard the news, I could not believe it.

What was hard for me to accept was that if as a child playing in the street with a piece of chalk I "knew" that a sailor was going to come home so unexpectedly, why did I not pick up a far more serious event, when walking in the same area before an event with such dire heart breaking consequences? Perhaps it was fate. I do honestly feel that this incident more than all the other atrocities filled people with revulsion for the IRA. This, too, was the incident I am sure I had been told would happen involving children and then people would begin to change. Southern Ireland made it known that the IRA had nothing to do with them. Peace marches started. It started an echo throughout the world especially America. America began to intervene. Warrington was not a legitimate target. It was a small town remote from anything to do with Irish politics. The children were innocents and the sight of them lying mangled on that Spring morning in that northern street convinced people that mattered that they had had enough.

Bombings and slayings in Belfast and London people had become inured to. In Belfast and Ulster itself for that matter, it was endured and almost accepted as normal. Nice, decent, ordinary Irish people, put the fear of the terrorists to the back of their minds and stood up to the IRA saying "Your are not acting for me!" It was a start.

I had developed a routine at this time of Absent Healing sessions. I would meditate daily to music and would concentrate intently on the map of Ireland. I had been taught that to send Healing mentally one had to fill the mental image with a great white light. I got quite expert at this. I would fill every corner of Ireland with light and love. At times flocks of white doves flew out of the centre. Now that I was no longer based in Ulster this was my way of fighting the horror of fanatic terrorism. I had to do something when the 'Trick or Treat' murders occurred at the Rising Sun in Greysteel. I asked the Colonel if there was any way that I could go back. I had friends in Greysteel. The slaughter just went on. Other people were doing my job now, so it was not possible for me to go. I did not like it but I had to accept it. I carried on with the Absent Healing sessions. Near to the barracks was a lovely little village called Ashwell. A major was sent on a temporary posting to Belize and I lived for a few months in her house whilst she was away.

In the ancient Church there was a board with little handwritten cards asking for Healing and Help. I put one of mine with the others. Dear God, please help to bring peace to Northern Ireland. These thoughts filled my life. Many millions more were doing the same thing I am sure, as I found the next time I wandered into the empty Church during a tour around the village. Two Irish ladies were kneeling at the Altar saying the Rosary aloud even though it was not a Catholic Church.

It was on my walk around the village of Ashwell ten years after I had first experienced it, that the second of my two visions became clear to me. I was walking across a bridle path in a field and I came across the chestnut horses nudging each other playfully whilst galloping friskily obviously enjoying every moment of their game. Every blade of grass, every colour was as vivid and as clear as it had been on that morning when I uncannily had foreknowledge of this very moment as I stood in this field feeling the very same thoughts that I thought then, of how undescribably beautiful this scene was. It was a surreal beauty. I have never seen anything quite so magnificent as those horses - it was as if they were performing especially for me.

The first vision had also taken ten years to present itself. It was the scene in the Gulf War that I had seen as I was about to leave for Northern Ireland. I took it as a marker for this event. No words were spoken on that occasion.

In this second vision I recognised the horses but the brown robed monk did not then become apparent to me. I had seen the horses first and then the monk. This part of the experience did not materialise until some time later in very unusual surroundings.

I went on holiday to Greece some weeks later to a remote area not far from Llindos and to the Island of Symi. I was overwhelmed with the beauty and the ancient history of Greece and of man itself for that matter. It was quite a spiritual trip for me. It was hard to feel spiritual in an Army Barracks. One only has to walk alongside the Parade Square and wince at the foul language and bellowing commands to feel grounded.

In Greece on that holiday mentally and spiritually I just soared as I took in the sights and sounds of this ancient civilisation.

Being in a remote area in a Studio that was little more than a Monks Cell with bed, chair, table, and wardrobe, with no distractions whatsoever I spent many hours in meditation with a walkman and 'Enya' for company.

It is hard for me to describe exactly what happened there but during the Absent Healing sessions when again I concentrated on the map of Ireland something almost superhuman seemed to be happening. The light that came seemed purer, deeper, more filled with love than it ever had before. I was overcome at the intensity of it. I can understand why clerics spend time in Retreat and isolation. I certainly spent much time alone although I did swim and walk the mile and half into the village sometimes for evening dinner. It was a rare opportunity to tune myself into the serenity and peace that comes from good meditation. It is a little hard to do that in an Army Barracks.

I enjoyed Greece so much that in July I decided to go on a tour to Italy. Not a lot of time to spend in Meditation there. It was a tour with lots of exciting things to see. Again it was magic. Rome, Florence, Venice, Sorrento. It was magnificent. I felt so lucky to be able to do this. It was in Assisi, reputed to be the religious centre of the world, that part two of my second vision emerged.

I have to stress here that I do not go for organised religion. If I visit a church I visit any church. I believe in a source of goodness (call it God or whatever). That source is available to all. Rather like an orange with lots of different slices but it all originates from the one whole. That is my conception of GOODNESS or GOD.

Anyway, as I was walking casually through the courtyard of the Church of Assisi, unexpectedly I came across the exact same figure of the monk that had been in my vision. I stared at him. His back view was again uncannily the same. He turned and looked straight at me. I smiled and he gave a returning smile. That was it!

In my vision he had been swathed in layers of bandages. One layer, then another and another. I remembered after each layer I had expected to see the face but always there was another layer until finally a corrupt sore filled face was exposed and then the face changed into something beautiful. The face of the monk that I had just seen. Obviously symbolically it meant something but quite what it was I was not sure. it was very puzzling.

When I returned to England I had received a Posting Order to go to Germany. Only a matter of weeks before the IRA entered negotiations for peace and TV news bulletins showed Irish and American politicians together with Gerry Adams announcing their intent.

The layers of bandages denoted the number of weeks, I am sure now, to the day that these announcements were made, of that I am convinced. Tim Parry's head was swathed in bandages as he lay mortally wounded in Warrington. The words that were spoken were:

You have had to face incredible misfortune. This will now be put right through Divine inspiration and your guideline to this will be the American political scene.

America has played a vital role in bringing these events about. Pressure has been put on the IRA to denounce violence and promise of financial support if efforts are made for peaceful negotiations. I am sure that they have played a more vital role than they will every be given credit for by the British who feel that it is none of their business.

Like me, third generation Irish, there are millions in American the same, all feeling the same anguish over the barbarity of the last twenty odd years. Many, many people have contributed to the jigsaw that brought these efforts about. Each has put a little piece in. I hope that I managed to put a piece in too and we must never allow these fanatical, cruel, violent people to start again on their twisted campaign that has robbed so many families of their loved ones.

The world is such a small place now that most of us have originated from somewhere else. Let us all remember that when the question of territory becomes an issue that causes conflict.

It is time that we all learned to love one another.

I have no wish now to stay in Germany. My family need me. I feel that I have been relieved of a great burden. It is not over yet but please God it will be. I have grandchildren whom I have rarely seen during my six years now with the British Army. A new child is expected soon. All I wish now is to go home to them.

The soldiers who are 'my boys' now are preparing to go to another conflict in Bosnia. I wish them well and tell them that I will miss them. But Bosnia is not my war! There are other people who will agonise and pray over that.

Germany - snow shovelling

64

For me the war is over! Even in fact, if it is not.

As I look back to those long gone days in Caroline Street as I played hopscotch and wrote uncannily of a future event when I wrote 'Welcome Home Pat Ruane', I did not realise that it would take me on such a personal crusade that would involve such wonderful experiences.

Now, I want to go HOME!

A year later I was posted home. Only twenty miles from my mother and sisters and brother. Not too far either from my daughter, Lesley, and five grandchildren.

For a while I was relieved about the ceasefire - just happy to be with my family.

New incidents occurred - 'Old habits die hard' unfortunately and peace talks broke down. Peace was by no means secure and tension crept back into Ulster.

Ordinary people in Northern Ireland had enjoyed the brief respite and were loathe to go back to the bad old days. It is the posturing, pontificating politicians and the criminal element who enjoy terrorism who need to change their ways. Please God it will not go back to what it once was. We must all make sure that it does not.

I still send a Healing light. The only contribution I can make. It is for others to negotiate to find the right formula to reach an agreement. No easy matter at all!

I cannot complete this story without a final tribute to my mother, Nora Gleavey nee McCarthy. It was so lovely for a change to have access to Mam. Her body was becoming frail although her spirit was still indefatigable. On a late summer day I was out shopping with her in Widnes. We pottered happily around the market stalls content with each other's company when she fell awkwardly and broke her arm. Distressed at her pain I took her to hospital and at first we all thought that she would be fine. Heartbreakingly she developed pneumonia and was very ill for three weeks. Five of us, her children, spent days and nights around her bed anxiously caring for her. It was the hardest thing that any of us has ever had to do. We loved and admired her so much for all the work and sacrifices that she had made for us. Her hard life had been lived with such fortitude.

She began to dream vividly of her sister, Molly, who had died when still young. Mam never really got over her death. They had been so close after they had both been widowed young. I did not discuss the Paranormal with my mother. At one time she feared it but she did have a few Psychic episodes of her own.

Some years ago, when babysitting for my younger sister Julie, a grill pan on the cooker in the kitchen had burst into flames. At first she stood rigid with shock wondering what to do when she felt a strong push towards the sink. She heard my father's voice telling her not to panic, just to wet the tea towel and lay it over the flames. She did as he said, although he had been dead for over twenty years at this stage. When my sister came home Mam was white faced and quiet and did not tell her about my father. She had been so shocked that a week went by before she told anyone.

Quite recently she told us that one morning she awoke early and felt that someone was lying alongside her in the bed at her back. She was just about to get out of bed when she heard my father say "Oh, don't get up yet Nora, it's too early". This time she was not afraid she told us quite matter of factly. I said that it was nice that he was still looking after her after all this time but my sister, Nora, was alarmed and did not like it at all. As she lay getting weaker and weaker in the hospital, with all my heart I wanted to tell her not to be afraid, just to go towards the light and she would find Molly.

My sisters and brother tried desperately to get her to hold on to life. None of us wanted to let her go. We implored her to get well, that she must'nt give up. She tried but she was so weary. She said "I am going to go to sleep soon". Towards the end when I was alone with her I told her "You will soon be with Molly and all your family again Mam". She was one of thirteen children and was the last to survive. I just sat and gently stroked her hair. To our great sadness she died quietly soon afterwards.

We were all devastated. Life would never be the same for any of us ever again. I remember once reading "Her diamonds and pearls were her boys and girls" and we certainly were hers. She did us proud and she left us with an emptiness that will never again be filled. It was hard to come to terms with a life without Mam. She had been the mainstay of our lives for so long. She had endured a hard life and had given us so much with her quiet, gentle unselfishness. I think that we all took stock of our lives.

Now that I was in my home area again I knew that when I was able to retire from my work that I wished to do so, in spite of the fact that I could choose to stay for another five years. Four grandchildren had been born whilst I had been working for the Army and I had seen very little of them. They gave me a lot of joy. With this in mind I decided to rent a cottage ready for my retirement only ten minutes drive away from my daughter Lesley and five grandchildren and only forty-five minutes drive from Widnes. It was in beautiful surroundings, tranquil, yet not too remote and I half formed plans for future Psychic work.

As I negotiated terms the Colonel of my Regiment asked if I would like to go with them on a six week Exercise to East Africa. There then following a mad whirl of shopping for lightweight clothing and a rush for the vital injections.

The soldiers teased me unmercifully about snakes and scorpions, mosquitoes and numerous other horrors including brothels and tales of genitalia dropping off. I must have been the only one in the British Army Tour that they didn't have to worry about on that score. The Quartermasters Department fitted me out with two sets of Combat Uniform for when I was in the jungle (not if I could help it). I had water bottles, mosquito net, sweat rags and a huge Bergen to put on my back. They put the Bergen on my shoulders and even with it empty I sank to my knees and fell over. They thought that it was great and laughed heartily.

Mam - Xmas 1996

Sister Julie and Ann - Xmas 1996

Goldie Hawn in 'Private Benjamin' I was not. I was over the hill and off the pill and rapidly approaching my bus pass. I'd go in my own style or not at all.

The Regiment collected together on the Parade Ground with their Bergens and Sleeping Mats awaiting the transport to Brize Norton for the flight to Nairobi. Between the rows of soldiers all standing to attention I tried unobtrusively, scarlet faced to walk pushing a civilian suitcase with loudly squeaking wheels, clutching my handbag and a violently coloured Argos sleeping bag under my arm. "Not very Military Mary" jeered a young Officer as he threw my luggage on to a four tonner. I groaned inwardly and hoped that I would not let myself and the Regiment down. I could make a right fool of myself.

I had been told to expect the very worst in living conditions at Nanyuki, the base camp in Kenya. I would be sleeping on concrete or on the earth floor. Washing facilities would be primitive but I must admit that the Padre put the wind up me when he asked quite seriously "Mary, are you allowed to bear small arms to protect yourself from wild animals?" As the only wild animals I had come across were the soldiers in the NAAFI, I didn't feel very confident.

On arrival at Nairobi my first view of a Third World country made me feel ashamed at all the terrible poverty. Even the most lowly paid of us lived in luxury compared to these people. As we drove through towns and villages children ran alongside the bus calling through the open windows for treats. Good humourdly the soldiers threw all that they had but it was little enough. The roadside shacks were dilapidated. The market stalls displayed meagre fruit and vegetables. I wondered how on earth that they all lived. It was an eye opener.

We arrived exhausted at the Base Camp after hours of groaning and jostling over rough roads. I was gratified to find that I had been allocated a fairly large Army tent with an old Army bed on a concrete base with wardrobe and chest of drawers. The Hilton, no less!

I need not have worried. We were too high up in altitude at Nanyuki for mosquitoes. Afternoons were hot but the mornings and evenings were cool and pleasant and I had no trouble at all in avoiding the 'Bawdy Houses'. Most afternoons I would walk down town to Nanyuki to look at wood carvings with three or four soldiers walking around me for protection as robbery was common place. Local people seemed intrigued by this silver haired lady in Army Combats surrounded by her guard. They came to the conclusion that I was 'The Queen' and thought it all very quaint indeed.

With the Padre I visited local schools and an orphanage and we came across a ten year old boy who was severely 'tongue tied'. His tongue was solidly stuck to the base of his mouth. He had never spoken properly and eating was very difficult for him.

The Royal Engineers were building a new school as an Army Project so I decided to have a project of my own. I collected money from the boys in the Regiment and one day I picked up Thomas and his mother and baby sister and took them to the hospital for Thomas to have an operation at the Cottage Hospital. The taxi was held together with string and it was some journey but Thomas was in good spirits and very excited. The operation was successful and as I took him back very tired and very sleepy to his home all the neighbours came out smiling and clapping from their very primitive shacks. A lump came to my throat. It didn't seem such a big thing to do but for these people it was everything.

Before we came away we left enough money for another child to be helped in a similar way. At least I felt that in a country with so much need we had done something to help.

In a matter of weeks Thomas was singing and chattering and eating almost normally.

The soldiers were very busy on Exercise of course so I was left to my own devices a lot of the time. I was allowed to go off on Safari with an American lady doctor. 'Daktari' the locals called her. She was an amazing character utterly devoted to her work with the poor. She made me feel very humble.

Doctor Margery and I set off one morning at the crack of dawn and I have never had such an adventure. Her driving was erratic and I spent half of it with my hands over my eyes. We had to go to Nairobi first to pick up some supplies and I must admit that a few times I did feel seriously threatened as we made necessary stops in African territory. The looks we got were hostile and threatening with the threat of robbery and violence every present.

We escaped unscathed however until we arrived near dusk at the Nakuru Wildlife Area. The Jeep's wheels got stuck in impacted sand. The vehicle decided that it had had quite enough and so had we. Nervously with Margery at the wheel I tried to dig us out, all the time looking over my shoulder for lions - or buffalo, which Margery said were worse. It was no use, we couldn't move. We sat tight hoping that someone would come along to help. Eventually Margery's friends came looking for us and we were very relieved to be pulled out of the sand by a four tonner.

After a meal and a beer around the camp fire, filthy and encrusted in dust but too exhausted to wash, I crawled into a tiny one-man tent telling myself that it really was about time that I settled down at my age and with crossword and the WI and not playing Mrs Indiana Jones in East Africa.

Within minutes the camp was in an excited turmoil as a Pride of Lions could be heard roaring nearby. I was to tired I couldn't move and I thought "Oh, well, if they get me, they get me" and I stayed put. Fortunately for me the lions attacked and killed a poor impala and the camp settled again for the night. Just as I was drifting off I heard someone shout "Don't use the Toilet Tent tonight, there is a leopard on the prowl!" I had a cast iron bladder that night.

During that few days we saw all the wildlife that there was to see and it was amazing. I felt so lucky to be having this experience. Margery and I visited bush villages and she treated the patients and under her instructions I dispensed the medicines. If it was a child I slipped a sweet in with the pills.

We laughed a lot especially with her friends, a group of people from Guernsey who were building a school. Doctor Margery asked me as we drove back if I would like to stay out in Kenya to help her and touched as I was by Africa's needs I knew that I would have to say no. I couldn't just abandon my family completely to do that. My dedication lay always in Northern Ireland and I felt that many others would help Africa.

My trip to Kenya with the Regiment turned out to be the trip of a life-time. It was hard and arduous in parts especially the travelling in Army

Orphanage at Nanyuki

Thomas Kinyui, Mother and Teachers in Africa

Africa - at the wheel

trucks across boulder strewn territory with no roads. I felt rather like a kaleidoscope that had been shaken violently and all the bits of me had come back down in different places. I wouldn't admit this, however. I smiled brightly to assure the lads that I was all right if they looked at me concerned.

Somehow, as they pulled back the roof and we stood balancing precariously with our heads and shoulders out watching a herd of magnificent elephants pass in front of us it was worth every discomfort. I think that I even surprised myself!

A trip by helicopter to Lake Navaisha, the Adventure Training Area, was much easier on my old bones. Two Army Corp boys treated me like a VIP as they flew me over the breathtakingly beautiful Aberdare Mountains. It was all such wonder to me.

I spent one guilty night in the face of so much struggle and poverty at the Mount Kenya Safari Hotel, reputed to be the best in the world and owned by Al Fayed of Harrods' relatives. I luxuriated in the sunken bath and sumptuous surroundings complete with four poster bed. Dinner was nine beautifully arranged courses. Although I felt thoroughly pampered, one night was enough for someone who quite likes egg and chips!

I came away from Kenya feeling the luckiest of people.

During my stay at the Mount Kenya Hotel I recalled a vivid dream that I had experienced some years before when I had been looking through the window of a building at the spectacular beauty of a lush panoramic view. it was quite the most perfect scene that I have every seen in my life. It was the very view from the Mount Kenya Safari hotel. I could only marvel at it and wonder had fate brought me there and if so why. Was it a reward for something? If it was, I was so genuinely thankful.

All I wanted now was to be with my family and move into my cottage to begin a new life, one in which I would give talks to people to tell them of my experiences. Maybe people would even want to read about them. Money would be tight but that had never stopped me before.

So, roll on old age I'm not quite ready for it but resigned to it. Something will turn up - probably!

74

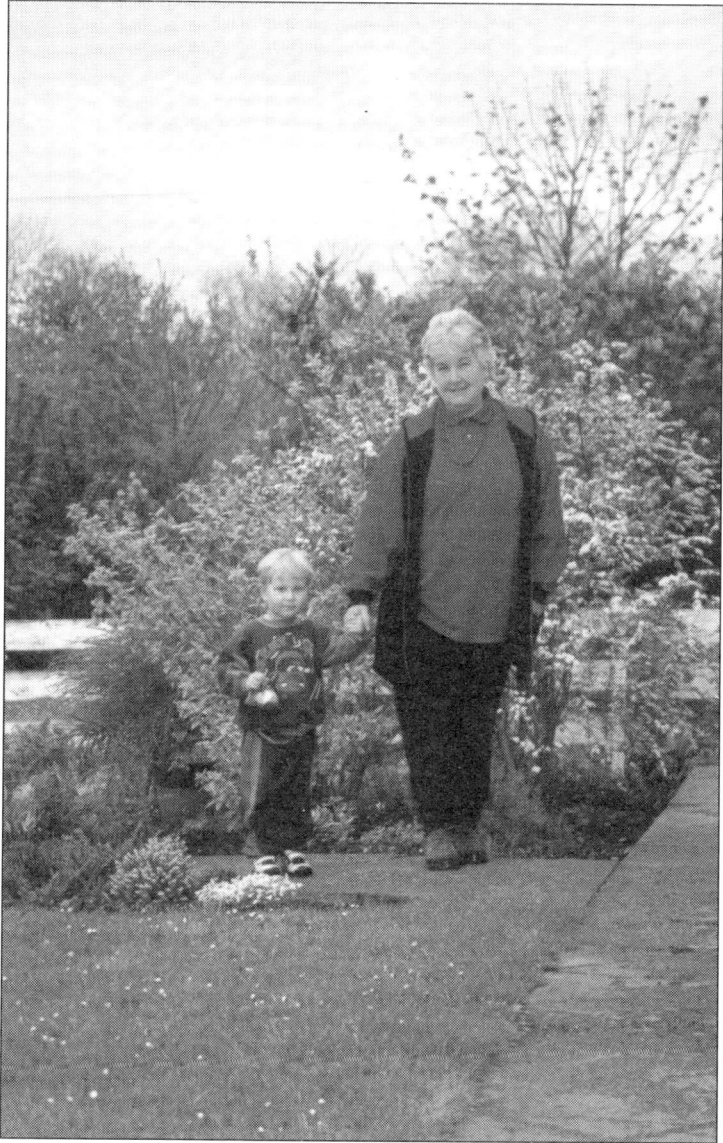

Myself and Grandson Jesse in Wales.